The bilingual experience

The bilingual experience

A book for parents

EVELINE DE JONG

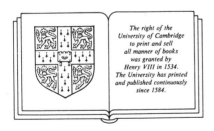

*The right of the
University of Cambridge
to print and sell
all manner of books
was granted by
Henry VIII in 1534.
The University has printed
and published continuously
since 1584.*

CAMBRIDGE UNIVERSITY PRESS

Cambridge
London   New York   New Rochelle
Melbourne   Sydney

Published by the Press Syndicate of the University of Cambridge
The Pitt Building, Trumpington Street, Cambridge CB2 1RP
32 East 57th Street, New York, NY 10022, USA
10 Stamford Road, Oakleigh, Melbourne 3166, Australia

First published 1986

Printed in Great Britain by the
University Press, Cambridge

British Library cataloguing in publication data
De Jong, Eveline D.
The bilingual experience: a book for parents.
1. Bilingualism   2. Children—Language
3. Psycholinguistics
I. Title
306'.4   P115

Library of Congress cataloging in publication data
Jong, Eveline D. de.
The bilingual experience.
Bibliography: p.
1. Bilingualism.   2. Parenting.   I. Title.
P115.J66   1985   404'.2   85 – 19498
ISBN 0 521 31744 4

UP

Contents

Contents

Preface

This book deals with the decisions to be made and the emotional problems faced by parents who want to raise their children in a bilingual home environment. In doing so, it draws upon the real-life experiences of parents, whether or not they have succeeded in bring up their children to be bilingual. Basically, it is a book for parents – and others – by parents.

Not so long ago bilingualism was regarded as a handicap, as it was associated with minority groups and as bilingual children were considered to do less well at school. Nowadays, a bilingual upbringing seems rather more accepted as one of the many optional or necessary features in children's lives. One even gets the impression that bringing up one's children with two languages has become a fashionable thing to do, and a bilingual upbringing is now often regarded as some kind of key to success in our internationally oriented society.

The category of bilingual families is a growing one. Moreover, these days an increasing number of the parents involved want to make a conscious decision whether or not to preserve their mother tongue at home. And, if they decide to teach their children their own language, they still want to make sure that the children do well at school and in their social life. This book enables parents to compare their own experiences with those of other parents who have brought up their children in a bilingual home environment. It will also help those new parents who are considering a bilingual upbringing for their children to choose their own priorities and to make informed decisions, bearing in mind the interests of their children and of themselves as mothers and fathers.

Many factors play a role when parents decide whether or not they want their children to speak two languages, but the advice they receive from other bilingual parents that they happen to meet will not always apply to their particular needs. As a result, they may begin to feel isolated in a situation which is common to so many people all over the world. In all, from the moment I myself began to think and talk about the bilingual upbringing of my children, it took me well over a year to find an example that really matched my own situation and that helped me to choose my own direction. Yet I believe that people who know most about the problems of living with two languages are those who are actually in that situation themselves. They provide the best source of information for other parents looking for advice. And if it is rare to find one particular case that exactly resembles one's own, the combined experiences of parents will tell the reader what life is like in a bilingual home environment.

The people whose experiences are described in this book are mostly of European origin and have migrated within Europe. They have all settled in their new country on a more or less permanent basis. But the subject matter will also appeal to other bilingual families, whether they have migrated outside Europe – in particular to Canada, the USA, or Australia – or whether they have planned a temporary stay in a foreign country.

Parents and their children are the main participants in a bilingual upbringing, and the book directs itself primarily to parents. But bilingual families are not an isolated group and therefore the book should be of concern to anyone interested in the phenomenon of bilingualism, whether they are relatives or whether they are professionally involved with children, such as schoolteachers or workers in the psychological and medical fields.

Acknowledgements

My first word of thanks must go to my mother, who suggested the subject of this book in the first place.

I am very grateful to Annie Cave, Pamela Davidson, Rosemary Davidson, Anne Green, Jan Magnus, Christine Park, Kirsten Williams, and Betsy Zander. They all read drafts of various stages of the book, and I greatly benefited from their critical comments and their encouragement.

Many thanks are due to Dieuwke, who looked after me and my family so very well during the year that I carried out the interviews and wrote the book. Her presence downstairs enabled me to keep on working upstairs.

And, of course, I am immensely grateful to the parents I interviewed. Not only were they always very welcoming and hospitable, but each of the more than fifty conversations was an enjoyable and stimulating occasion. Equally, I am indebted to those twenty parents who returned the questionnaire to me by post – and almost all promptly, too!

I cannot name all the parents who helped me along, but special thanks to Angelika Sahla, Anja Hoffman, Jonneke Gerritsen, Lotte and Hugh Shankland, Theresa Michel, and Natalia Benjamin. Without the time and energy given to me by them, by all the other parents, and by a dozen of their teenage children, this book would not have come about.

My thanks to you all.

1
Searching for information

❝When I moved with my husband and our eight-month-old baby from Amsterdam to Vancouver, the matter of a bilingual upbringing was among the least of my worries. Our life was too much taken up by the practical issues of moving house and settling in Canada to have much scope for contemplating the language development of Gideon.

It wasn't until he was almost four years old and still showed very few signs of learning any English – in spite of first having been going to a day-care centre and later to a playgroup for more than two years altogether – that we had to acknowledge that bringing up one's child with two languages is not just a matter of course, that it might pose too many problems for the child involved, and that we had to make a conscious decision as to whether or not we wanted to keep up our mother tongue at home.

By that time, we had had our second child, we had moved to London, and we had settled there on a more or less permanent basis. People started suggesting to us that we should give up speaking Dutch, at least to the children, thus making it easier for them to adapt to the English-speaking surroundings. So far we have rejected that possibility and we still speak Dutch with our children, but at times we feel that we have to defend ourselves for doing so!❞

Sources of information

Why isn't a bilingual upbringing just a matter of course? And how does that correspond to the fact that millions of children all over the world grow up with two languages, seemingly without problems? And, as for the advice and comments that I receive from people around me, why do they never seem to be quite to the point? In short, what is known about bilingual children?

An obvious place to look for answers to these questions was in books, and I began my search for information by consulting the child-care manuals on my shelf that had helped me during the early years of parenthood. However, I found that on this subject the books were silent. Is growing up with two languages still regarded as exceptional? Or does it just happen 'naturally', so that there is no need to write about it?

1

I found another source of information in the existing academic case studies of bilingual children. These case studies supplied me with a wealth of linguistic detail, but they didn't deal with any of the sorts of problems that we and our children were experiencing. Moreover, they typically reported on 'success stories', often describing children of parents who themselves were linguists, and I felt that these studies had very little to offer me. I was trying to find out more about the day-to-day issues that arise in a bilingual home environment.

I also asked parents in a similar situation about their experiences. The problem with bilingualism, however, is that there are so many variations on the theme. This is true for practically all the issues parents face when bringing up their children but I felt it more acutely with regard to the bilingual situation. When seeking advice from other bilingual families I found that their position was never quite the same as my own: they had come for a short stay only, or they had migrated quite a long time ago; the parents involved spoke a different foreign language; they had a much better, or worse, command of the local language; the children had been born in the country where the family was now living, or when the family had 'moved' countries their children were much older than mine.

Still, I decided to press on with interviewing other parents, and I also sent questionnaires (containing the same questions as were asked during the interviews) to those people I couldn't visit personally. Gradually a picture emerged of parents and children who were experiencing a bilingual situation that was similar to my own, and it was from all these families taken together that I learned most about all the issues that can play a role in a bilingual upbringing.

Parents and children

Parents and children are the two main parties involved in a bilingual upbringing and both parties of course have plenty to say on the subject. Being a parent myself, I was first and foremost interested in the experiences of other parents who were right in the middle of bringing up their children with two languages. Parents, of course, would be able to supply information on the reactions and problems of their children as well as on their own dilemmas and decisions.

I was also interested in hearing from the other party concerned – the children – so I thought it would be useful to talk to adults who had grown up bilingually. By coincidence, when I first embarked upon my search for information, I seemed to meet quite a few of them. They were always very willing to share their memories with me, but, apart from the fact that memories tend to become unreliable with the passing of time, the somewhat vague childhood recollections didn't reveal very much about how the situation as a whole was dealt with, let alone how it was experienced by their parents.

So I decided not to include their accounts in this book and instead to rely on present-day parents as my informants on the subject of a bilingual home environment. Very interestingly, however, through the stories of those people who had experienced a bilingual childhood in the past, it gradually became clear to me that the situation in which they had grown up with two languages was usually rather different to that of children in bilingual families today. One observation in particular made me realize the differences that are involved.

Gertrud, who is now in her fifties, came to England in the 1930s and she, like many others, grew up with two languages. She told me:

'One thing we all learned from a very young age onwards was to act as interpreters for our parents.'

When I heard this, my reaction was: 'But up till now, I have always had to act as an interpreter for my children!' Why was their situation so different from my own? The answer is that one of the reasons why people become bilingual is migration and people move abroad for different reasons. Broadly speaking, one could call it a difference between compulsory and voluntary reasons. On the one hand there were and still are many families who migrate in order to escape from war, poverty, and unemployment. On the other hand there are growing numbers of people, especially within Europe, who move abroad because of marriage or a career, or because of the plain wish to widen their horizons.

People who move abroad of their own free will have different aims when settling in a new country than those who are forced to migrate. Compulsory migration often means that one either tries to integrate oneself and one's children into a new country and a new culture, or – as is also often the case – isolates oneself from it. People who have moved voluntarily often aim at combining the different influences, such as culture, food, and, of course, languages. While in the case of forced migration the bilingual situation is one that just has to be coped with, parents who have migrated without having been compelled to do so often actively wish their children to become bilingual. This made me realize that it is worth making a distinction between children who are growing up bilingually and children who are brought up bilingually.

Growing up bilingually versus a bilingual upbringing

For those who live in the Western world, where monolingualism rather than bilingualism seems to be the norm, it often comes as a surprise

3

that – as estimated by linguists – at least half the world's population is bilingual. Often the reason for bilingualism is migration, but even more often the language spoken at home is not the same as the one spoken outside because of political, economic, or geographical reasons. Sometimes several official languages exist side by side in one area or one country. Sometimes a language is imposed as the official one for public life, while different ethnic groups cling to their own languages in their home environment.

A common characteristic of all these situations is that the children growing up in them will have to adjust to the bilingual or multilingual environment. If the parents also come from a multilingual background, it might well be that living with two or more languages has become a way of life over a number of generations. However, in the case of forced migration or in the case of recent political and economic changes within a country, parents usually know only one language, while the children have to learn a different one at school. But whatever the cause may be, growing up bilingually means that there is no choice: for the children and parents concerned it is a fact of life and they will have to cope with it as well as they can.

A bilingual upbringing, on the other hand, is an option that can be considered by those parents who have migrated to a new country on a voluntary basis and who are already reasonably fluent in two languages before they have to start contemplating the bilingual upbringing of their children. There are many permutations but two general groups fall into this category: partners who have moved abroad together and have a common mother tongue ('single-language marriages'), and people who have migrated on their own and have married someone who has a different mother tongue ('mixed-language marriages'). Provided both partners – or at least one of them in a mixed-language marriage – are more or less bilingual, these couples can make a conscious decision to bring up their children bilingually.

In practice the choice isn't always straightforward. There are many degrees of fluency in a foreign language, and there are numerous circumstances which will influence the decision. But the main difference between growing up bilingually and being brought up bilingually is that the parents involved have chosen to create and to maintain the bilingual situation as opposed to a situation where parents and children just have to adjust to it in order to survive.

This book is concerned with the issues of a bilingual upbringing rather than with growing up in a bilingual environment. It does not describe families who are bilingual because they live in a part of a country where a minority language is being spoken next to a national language (e.g. Welsh–English or Frisian–Dutch families), or because they live in a country such as Switzerland or Belgium where several national languages exist side by side. This book describes the experiences of those parents who – by moving abroad – have created a bilingual home environment for themselves and their children, and who are in a position to make choices with respect to the bilingual upbringing of their children.

Temporary or permanent settlement

When talking about parents who are faced with the choice of a bilingual upbringing for their children, we have to consider those who have moved on a temporary basis as well as those who have moved on a permanent basis. One important difference between those two groups is that parents who move temporarily can sometimes decide to avoid the bilingual issue altogether by leaving the children back home (boarding school), or by sending them to a local school where the curriculum is taught in the home language (French Lycée), or by enrolling them in an international school where they cater for children with many different mother tongues. This is especially true in the case of families of diplomats and employees of multinational companies or large international organizations, as funds are often made available to send the children to these schools.

Another difference in the bilingual situation between permanent and temporary residents is illustrated by the following remark. It was made by a Norwegian mother, whose husband was in the Norwegian diplomatic service. The couple lived in London with their small daughter for two years and she said this about the situation:

'I think it is very good for my daughter to become bilingual, for English is a very useful language to know. We hope to keep it up once we are back in Norway and it may also be helpful when we are posted to another country.'

These parents made the choice for their daughter to become bilingual, but it was a choice of a different kind. To them the question of keeping up Norwegian didn't even arise, only the usefulness of learning English. Parents who move abroad on a permanent basis can't choose whether or not their children should learn the language of the country of residence. The decision to be made by them is whether or not they want to keep up their original mother tongue.

Of course, the fact remains that many people do not know beforehand if their stay in a foreign country is going to be a temporary or a permanent one. It is not uncommon to begin with a two or three year stay, and only after this first period is the decision made to stay permanently or to go back. But I think that parents who are

5

contemplating a bilingual upbringing for their children – whether they have moved abroad temporarily or on a permanent basis – can learn most from the experiences of those families for which a bilingual home environment has become a permanent reality, in particular where the reactions of the children to the bilingual upbringing are concerned. And, while I only interviewed parents who had settled with their children on a more or less permanent basis, some of these had travelled around before they had decided to settle, others had made a move abroad during an in-between period, and again others had moved for the first time when the children were already a bit older. So the issue of moving abroad with children – and what it entails for their bilingual development – will crop up regularly on the following pages.

About this book

Let me conclude this introductory chapter with a comment made by Angelika, one of the parents I interviewed, for it touches on many of the issues that will be raised in this book. She said:

'At the beginning I thought it would be very nice if the children could be bilingual. I felt we owed it to them, ourselves, our friends, the middle class. The kinds of things we had to go on were only what I knew about children of diplomats and it was always said that they were all terrifically bilingual and able to speak seven or eight languages fluently. So I thought we should follow in their footsteps. Well, we didn't get very far, I must admit.'

Angelika's comments show that she made a conscious decision in favour of a bilingual upbringing for her children. But Angelika, like me, found there was little or no information of a practical kind available and she assumed – like everyone else – that it would all be just a matter of course. She also strongly implies that it wasn't that simple after all. Will this also be the conclusion of this book?

In a sense, yes, for to bring up one's children with two languages is not always easy. As a matter of fact, if my own two children had reacted as if learning two languages was indeed easy and natural, this book would never have been written. Yet, by the end of the book it will be evident that many parents find bringing up their children bilingually well worth the effort.

2

On being bilingual – the parents

❝ Since we came to live in London we have made many new friends. From the beginning we were introduced to lots of people and generally we have been made to feel very welcome. Yet our relatives and old friends back in Holland are not very far away, and we also go to see them or they come to see us quite frequently. And sometimes I begin to wonder whether it is in fact possible to do both things: to settle in a new country and to hang on to old ties. Will I not somehow get lost in the middle, losing out on both sides?

It's the same with the languages I use every day. I want to practise and improve my English as much as possible, but I also want to carry on speaking Dutch at home. And the same question arises: will I gain by having both languages, or will I end up with not having either properly? ❞

A bilingual upbringing begins with one or both parents being bilingual. But what does it mean 'to be bilingual'? The parents I interviewed found it quite difficult to define the term in just a few words, but they had some clear ideas on what it means to live with two languages. In this chapter I describe how they experience being bilingual. As we shall see, some of them tried to define some kind of standard, a degree of proficiency to be achieved in the foreign language. Others were rather more concerned with the emotional ties one can have with different languages.

To be bilingual: why and when?

Before introducing some of the parents and their views on life with two languages, I will explain why and when I myself first started to think about being bilingual.

❝ I learned several languages at school and later continued at university to be trained as a translator. However, at the time I never thought about the subject of bilingualism or regarded myself as a bilingual person. The languages that I was learning were technical chunks of knowledge, similar to what I had learned in mathematics or geography. Even when I was studying to become a translator and

I was speaking, reading, and writing a foreign language almost every day, I just considered the use of a different language as a professional skill. It wasn't until I had moved abroad and had to live with two languages that I began to think about the subject of bilingualism and also began to experience the emotional impact of a bilingual situation. **⟩**

For some people, however, proficiency in a language is always the important requirement. This may mean that they consider bilingualism to be a goal that cannot be reached. One person who expressed this view was John. He said:

'No, I am not bilingual, for I don't believe that such a thing exists. One can be entirely fluent in a foreign language, but one will never be able to express oneself equally well in both languages in all spheres of life.'

There were other parents who treated the matter rather more lightly and who called themselves bilingual, because 'I can express myself equally well in both languages', or because 'when I speak a language I think in that language and I don't translate from the one into the other', or 'I switch without thinking'.

Most people who have lived in a foreign country for a considerable period of time will get a reasonable command of the new language, but they won't necessarily feel that they have become bilingual. One of them is Marco, who comes from Italy and has married an English wife. He explained:

'We came to live in England eight years ago. At the time when we met, my wife's Italian was better than my English, and Italian has remained the language of the house. At my job I speak English, but I feel that for social purposes my English vocabulary is limited, also because a number of our friends are Italian. In my view you are bilingual when you speak a foreign language and other people don't realize straightaway that you are not a native speaker. I think that I fall short of that standard, but my wife certainly meets it.'

The emotional factor

When asked how they would define their own bilingualism, many parents also mentioned a variety of emotional factors that decided for them whether or not they considered themselves to be bilingual. Angelika's mother tongue is German. Her answer to the question whether she would describe herself as a bilingual person was:

'Well, I wouldn't. I describe myself as very fluent in English, but not bilingual. In fact, I don't really know what bilingual means, because when I speak English, even after twenty years and all the studying I have done in this country and all the reading, I do not have the same feeling for the language that I have for German. I very often just use English words without having any of the association of feelings and experiences that I have when I use German words – I suppose these associations come from early childhood experiences.'

And Angelika also noticed: 'You see. I can swear in English at great length. It doesn't mean anything to me, it is just an exclamation. It could be "ooo" or "aaaa", it is just letters. I know that now is the time when you ought to say something rude, but the word itself is not rude to me.'

It is clear that one's attitude to a new language can be expressed in many ways. Rosella put it this way:

'English has become my stepmother-tongue.'

And her smile indicated that she wasn't quite sure how much she liked this relationship.

Fred, on the other hand, had one of the most positive views of bilingualism that I came across. He is Dutch and he has a French wife. They met and got married in France, but they have lived in Holland for eight years now.

'To be bilingual gives me a sense of power and achievement. Also, I find it relaxing: when I get home from a long day's work and can switch to speaking French instead of Dutch, it almost feels like going on a holiday in France.'

The next comment was made by Janine, who moved to England from the French-speaking part of Belgium:

'I consider myself to be bilingual, because I understand English jokes.'

This sounds to me a pretty good reason for considering oneself bilingual, as humour is often closely bound up with language. But Janine also added:

'Although I understand English jokes, I don't always think they are funny.'

Gaby, for her part, told me that she considered herself to be bilingual Dutch–English, although:

'I don't always understand English jokes and my husband will often say, "I will explain later", for it usually concerns jokes that don't permit a public explanation. But I probably would have had the same problem, if I had remained in Holland and had just spoken Dutch.'

9

The bilingual experience

One person, two identities

❝ From time to time, speaking a foreign language has made me feel a bit insecure in my social contacts. I still experience this, although now less often than when I first started living abroad. It isn't that I don't feel competent enough in the other language. Rather, I wonder: is it because of what I said or how I said it that someone suddenly stares at me as if I have just arrived from outer space?

One problem is that, personally, I am not a very good actor and sometimes I think that one should be in order to speak foreign languages properly. I still try to speak English as if it were Dutch, which means that I talk too quickly and don't choose my words carefully enough. But, if I did slow down and talk more deliberately, it somehow wouldn't quite feel like me. ❞

My own experience is clearly different from that of one of the other parents. His mother tongue is also Dutch and he made the following remark:

'When I speak French I feel French, and when I speak English I feel English. Language can be an artistic expression of oneself, and I think the way you express yourself in another language is more important than speaking it flawlessly.'

There is definitely a link between language and identity which is well worth exploring if we really want to understand what it means to be bilingual. Do different languages represent different aspects of one individual? I am inclined to believe that there is some truth in this. Of course, it's not true to the same extent for everyone, and for some it's probably not true at all. And equally, it is also true that one can have different identities and play different roles within the scope of one and the same language.

However, one mother gave me a striking example of how her little daughter acted out different aspects of herself through using different languages. The use of an imaginary person or playmate is a well-known phenomenon in child psychology. This little girl used this 'technique' to come to terms with the fact that she was living with two languages and two different sets of values, and I think it shows as if through a magnifying glass something that applies to many bilingual people. Madelon, the mother, is Dutch, but she lives in England. This is what she told me about her daughter:

'Charlie must have been about two-and-a-half when one day she spotted a small English girl on a playground who seemed very well behaved and didn't dare to do any wild things. It appears that she also overheard the girl's name, which was Laura, and from then on she used this name to refer to her imaginary English counterpart. If she was

10

Charlie, she was a wild and naughty Dutch girl; if she was Laura, she was quiet and polite. By the way, it's quite probable that these two characters also reflected her noisy Dutch mum, and her calm and self-possessed English nursery teacher.

'With time we learned how to live with those two persons and they would even be used as a means to escape from unwanted situations. "Go and fetch Laura", I sometimes told Charlie if there seemed no other way to stop her making a nuisance of herself. Later on, Laura became super-Laura and grew out of reach. And when one day my daughter said to me: "She doesn't really exist, but don't tell anybody", I knew she was growing out of this phase.'

And what about the mother tongue?

All the comments quoted so far have focussed on the acquisition of a new language, and two factors have emerged as deciding for parents whether or not they consider themselves as bilingual: the emotional relationship with the new language and the proficiency obtained. But what about the fluency in one's mother tongue? Among all the different 'definitions' given by the parents I talked to, one of the most revealing was: 'Yes, I consider myself to be bilingual, because I'm still fluent in my mother tongue.'

When I first heard this answer to my question – 'Would you describe yourself as bilingual?' – I hadn't lived abroad long enough myself to personally experience the possible loss of one's mother tongue. And until then I had often thought that people who no longer seemed capable of speaking their own language easily and fluently were either just pretending or were a bit stupid. With time I have come to realize that keeping up one's own language isn't as easy as it seems. To be or to remain fluent in a language one needs practice and if one settles permanently in a new country with a new language such practice isn't always available.

Geneviève moved from France to England some twelve years ago and she is married to an Englishman. She described her situation quite expressively:

'When I came to England I started working for a British company. I was speaking English all day, in fact my job entailed talking all the time on the phone and so on. At the time I didn't have any French friends in England and I started forgetting my French to a certain extent, and every time I went back to France it took me a while to adapt again. Everybody was saying I was speaking French with an English accent; lots of words were escaping me.'

She wasn't the only one who had felt this happening to her. Many parents complained that their mother tongue had become rusty or that they had to search for words. This was certainly more true for those who were the only one in a marriage speaking the foreign language, as in Geneviève's case. But even couples who had migrated together noticed that the new language would stealthily begin to replace the old one, especially when they talked about experiences that belonged to the new life abroad, such as a job, a new area of studying, or children. The way a language can have the monopoly in certain areas of one's life is also illustrated by Greet's remark:

'I lived in Holland when I was a child. I have lived in England as a wife and mother. My Dutch is a child's Dutch, and my knowledge of English words is probably greater, for I use words in English that I may never have used in Dutch.'

Another comment to be heard was that language changes all the time and it is impossible to keep in touch with the new words and phrases entering a language. Angelina:

'A lot has changed in Spain since I left twenty years ago and the language has evolved accordingly. I simply do not have the vocabulary to talk about the new political situation. At first it felt a bit awkward but, as I go to Spain regularly, I feel I am catching up now.'

For some parents even accent had become a problem. Rudi has been married to an English wife for fifteen years now and they have always lived in England and spoken English together. He observed:

'When I am in Holland, people no longer recognize me as being Dutch. Nowadays I get more comments on my accent in Dutch than on my accent in English. I would need at least three weeks in Holland to learn proper Dutch again but, although I pay regular visits, they never last that long.'

A foreign accent

On one occasion, when I had come to interview a mother about how she was bringing up her children with two languages, I thought after about five minutes: 'This must either be the wrong address or I should have been talking to the father as the parent who comes from abroad, for the person I'm talking to must be an English native speaker.' We had just been chatting before starting with the actual interview, so I hadn't asked yet for details such as country of birth or date of migration. It turned out that this mother had moved to England from Poland in her early twenties and at the time hardly spoke any English. She had married an Englishman, who didn't speak her language, so they had always communicated in English.

For me, this was obviously one of the most amazing examples of someone speaking a foreign language with an accent that could not be distinguished from a native speaker's and it showed that one needs only one exception to disprove the rule that 'adults cannot learn to speak a foreign language with a native accent'. However, in general it is true that when speaking a foreign language most adults can immediately be detected as a non-native speaker by their accent. And if for some parents accent can become a problem in the mother tongue, one would expect that for many more parents it would present quite an obstacle in the foreign language. In answer to the question whether she would describe herself as bilingual, Anke wrote:

'In one way, yes, because I speak Greek as easily as Dutch. On the other hand, I only have to open my mouth and people will say to me, "Oh, you're a foreigner, aren't you?" That's not what I call being bilingual.'

I myself share this sense of frustration with Anke, and I am sure that there are many more like us. Sometimes it seemed that particularly those parents who had mastered quite a good accent would add: 'And of course I will never learn to speak without a foreign accent.' A bit surprisingly, however, I found that relatively few parents took accent into account when I asked them about their bilingualism. More often than not accent was completely omitted from consideration. Or, when people tried to judge their own degree of bilingualism, many appeared to consider their pronunciation less important than their fluency, their ability to think in the second language, and their feelings towards it.

On reflection I felt this was more than a bit surprising, for in discussions about bilingual children, a 'perfect' accent in two languages is often seen as one of the greatest rewards of a bilingual upbringing. Undoubtedly, someone who has been brought up with two languages is far more likely to have a native accent in both of them than someone who acquires a second language in later life, but the observations made by bilingual people themselves may indicate that accent is perhaps less important as a 'reward' than is sometimes suggested. And even for children, acquiring a native accent in two languages isn't always a completely straightforward process, as we will see in Chapter 6.

Learning the hard way

So far I have talked about 'being bilingual', but I believe that bilingualism is a process rather than a state: almost every day you come across a new expression in the second language, or you discover a subtle nuance you didn't know before. At the same time you need to make a constant effort to keep up the mother tongue if you want to try and prevent odd little mistakes from creeping in.

13

When you are in a learning process, you need helping along. How do native speakers react when someone tries to grapple with their language? People whose mother tongue is English may not be very interested in learning other languages themselves, but they are extremely used to other people learning to speak theirs. They will never laugh at your mistakes and they will allow you to muddle on, while waiting politely and patiently until you have found the right expression.

This is all very nice but it's not too helpful. At times I would like them to correct a mistake or help me find a word I am desperately looking for, but – with one or two exceptions – they simply never do. Also, in a conversation, native speakers of English don't always realize that you might have difficulties in understanding them, probably because few of them have ever tried to understand another language themselves.

The reaction can be quite different in another country. Take the Dutch for example. Dutch people are rather proud of their ability to speak foreign languages. On the other hand, they can't understand why someone would want to learn Dutch. Anyone wanting to learn Dutch in the Netherlands after having moved there from abroad might have a similar experience to Judy's:

'I had to make it clear to people that I absolutely wanted to learn Dutch. We took a crash course just before we moved to Amsterdam and made an effort to communicate in Dutch from the very beginning. But it's not easy. For one thing, people will always answer you in English if they possibly can. But you can ask them not to do that. Then they might tease you if you make a funny mistake. And once they have decided to speak to you in Dutch, some may resort to addressing you in an oversimplified manner, as if you were an idiot.'

I can't say what it is like in other countries or when other languages are involved but it seems that, when learning either English or Dutch as a foreign language, you should not expect too much help or sympathy from a native speaker. Whether you meet with polite silence or are ridiculed, you are out there on your own, learning the hard way.

Speaking and understanding, writing and reading

In this discussion of bilingualism, I have only referred to the ability to speak two languages. However, for a more accurate description one should distinguish between speaking and understanding on the one side, and writing and reading on the other.

Few people have equal abilities in all four skills in both languages. For one thing, it depends on how the language has been learned. For those parents who learned the second language via an academic approach at school, this may mean that reading and writing the language presents less difficulty than speaking it, especially when first arriving in the new country. People who pick up most of the new language after their arrival often acquire an excellent command of the spoken language, while their ability to read and write it may remain rather limited.

I was told by quite a few parents that when they spoke a second language they no longer translated from the one language into the other, but that this was still the case when for instance writing a letter. At the other end of the scale I came across people who said they had grown so accustomed to writing specialized papers in English that they could no longer really do the same thing in their mother tongue.

Understanding and reading – what are known as the passive skills – are usually considered to be easier than the active skills of speaking and writing. Yet, anyone can be caught out by the intricacies of a foreign language. As Angelika said:

'Even now I can come across a book in English where on each page there are about six words that I have never seen or heard before, which can be quite a distressing experience.'

Annick comes from France and has lived in England for many years now. She talks English fast and easily, in a way as if it were French. She said:

'I read more easily in French than I would in English. I find it more pleasant, probably because in some ways maybe it is less of a struggle, although reading in English doesn't appear to be a struggle on the surface.'

Even understanding a foreign language is quite difficult sometimes. Even after you have lived in a country for many years, a dialect or local accent can still present a problem, perhaps when you go out shopping, or even when you are in your own home watching television. Another difficulty can arise when you join a group of three or four people who are having a conversation. The speed of the talking, the jokes and colloquialisms may at times baffle even the most seasoned bilingual person.

‹ However, I have discovered for myself one big advantage of living with a foreign language: I find it easier to switch off. When I am working in a library, or when I am getting tired or bored at a party, I can regard the spoken word around me as mere noise that can be ignored at will. ›

3

Why parents opt for a bilingual upbringing

As I explained in Chapter 1, my definition of a bilingual upbringing is that the parents involved have chosen to create and to maintain the bilingual situation as opposed to a situation where parents and children just have to adjust to it in order to survive. In this chapter, I want to look at why and when parents decide on a bilingual upbringing.

Is it essential to resolve upon a course of action before the child is even born? What are the advantages of being bilingual? What happens in the case of a drastic change in circumstances, such as a divorce? The reasons why parents decide to bring up their children with two languages are manifold. And, as we shall see, there are also many ways in which the decision can come about.

Making a choice

❝ For me and my husband, a bilingual upbringing wasn't a conscious choice from the very beginning. We never thought about the matter very much until we noticed that our children weren't reacting very favourably to the fact that they had to cope with two different languages. Until then we had more or less considered the bilingual upbringing as a fact of life, because the language of communication between ourselves, and thus the language we spoke to our children, was not the language of the country where we lived.

Our children's difficulties forced us to think carefully about their bilingual upbringing, but we didn't change our course of action. We have now made a conscious decision to keep up the Dutch language, and this is still the language in which all four of us communicate most freely and easily at home. At the same time, we trust that by learning English in the outside world, and especially at school, our children will stand every chance of becoming native speakers of that language. ❞

There are also many parents who do sit down and give the matter considerable thought well before the birth of their first child. I found this particularly true for couples who have different mother tongues. In theory, couples with a mixed-language marriage are in a position to define the problem in advance, to weigh the advantages and disadvantages, and to assess the feasibility of a certain course of action. Of course, practice may prove to be different from theory and the original choice may need to be reconsidered. But these parents are very likely to have considered the pros and cons of a bilingual upbringing from the start.

Gaby is Dutch and her husband is English. They have lived in England since their marriage and their children are now five and two-and-a-half years old. Their common language is English. Gaby told me:

'We did think and talk about the possibility of a bilingual upbringing before the birth of our first child. I come from a bilingual background myself, but both of us felt it was a good idea to bring up our children with two languages and that we would have to do it from the very beginning. It was now or never. Also, we thought that the kind of mental training it involved for the children would benefit them.

'And if I had any doubts about the feasibility of it, they soon disappeared after the arrival of my first baby. I could never have talked to him in any other language but my own. As a new mother I had already enough to worry about, and therefore I didn't want to have to bother about speaking a foreign language or to wonder whether I was using the right words or sentence constructions. David understands Dutch, so he doesn't need to feel excluded when I am talking to the children, but he always speaks English to them himself. Our children have had a truly bilingual upbringing from the very beginning.'

So far the older one, a boy, has responded better than the little girl: he is capable of keeping the two languages separate and speaks both of them, while the girl understands both English and Dutch, but will only speak English. Of course, these children are still young and only time will tell whether the parents will be able to stick to their original plans.

Another mother, with two little daughters, described how she had come to her decision to speak her own language with them. Kerstin is Swedish and is married to an Englishman. Their two girls are now five and one. She wrote:

'It made a great difference to me when, not long before my first daughter's birth, I realized that I was going to speak Swedish to a Swedish child – I mean that I realized suddenly that the child would be as much Swedish as English. It then came totally naturally to me to speak Swedish to her. Until then I had unconsciously thought I would be speaking Swedish to an English child and that would have been much more difficult to keep up.'

Taking a risk

But how are we going to find out whether these decisions and procedures will have worked by the time the children have grown somewhat older? One way is to look at a different though similar case of a family with older children: here is a mother who took the decision to have two languages in the house quite some time ago.

Annick comes from France and she has lived in England for almost twenty years now. Her husband was born in Germany, but he was brought up in England. Their children are fifteen, thirteen, and ten years old. For all three of them English is the more important language, but they all speak French fluently. I asked her how and when she decided on a bilingual upbringing. This is what she answered:

'I actually thought about it before they were born. I had seen two examples in my immediate neighbourhood which helped me to decide: one family succeeded in bringing up their child with two languages right from the very beginning, and the other waited until the age of seven and then the child refused to speak French. My main reason for speaking French to them was that I knew that whatever I was going to do English was going to take over anyhow. So I thought, the more French I get into them the better. At the same time I was warned that a lot of children who speak two languages don't know either of them very well and can have all sorts of difficulties. But I was prepared to take the risk.'

Annick said she took a risk, but obviously she has succeeded in bringing up her children bilingually. Parents often worry about this: whether they are actually taking a risk and how great that risk is. The fact is that there is still not much known about the effects of a bilingual upbringing in the long run, for the bilingual input can never be singled out as the one cause of a person's achievement, or failure, in a certain area of life.

I think the important thing to remember is that the language development of a bilingual child is different from that of a monolingual child and that, as we will see in the following chapters, some problems may indeed arise. But we will also see that, if parents take their time and don't make a great fuss about it during some of the more difficult periods, a bilingual upbringing can be a happy experience for parents and children alike.

Visits and visitors

One reason why Annick and her family have been rather successful in maintaining both languages is that over the years they have spent almost all their holidays in France and have had a constant stream of French visitors to their house in South London. As a matter of fact, practically all parents mentioned this as an important reason for embarking on a bilingual upbringing: the children should be able to communicate with the relatives who live abroad.

Travelling is now comparatively easy and cheap, and I found that many families see their relatives quite regularly, either visiting the original home country of one or both parents or having visitors from abroad. There often seems to be a smaller or larger group of people 'back home', consisting of relatives and friends, with whom we want to stay in touch. Some of our friends will get by in one or two foreign languages, but many of them don't. And the grandparents and cousins will usually speak only one language, while they are often the people that parents want their children to become particularly close to.

Rosella is Italian and lives in England, married to an Englishman. I am sure that she spoke for many other parents when she said:

'I wanted my children to have a close relationship with the grandparents on both sides. And I realized that they could only love their Italian grandmother in the same way they loved their English grandmother if they could feel comfortable when speaking Italian.'

She then continued:

'It has worked for my daughter, who is the eldest of my three children. She is now eight years old and although English is her best language, she will speak Italian to my mother, who stays with us in England regularly. But my four-year-old son has declared that he finds Italian too difficult to speak. Also, all the cousins who live in Italy happen to be girls, so he tends to stick to his father a great deal when we are there.'

Not only do parents want their children to be able to communicate with the grandparents, but parents also hope that grandparents will provide a natural impetus for the children to practise the foreign language, as Kaśka pointed out to me. She and her husband are yet another example of a mixed-language marriage: Kaśka comes from Poland, her husband is Dutch and they live in England, just outside London. Their language of communication is English, but Kaśka has been speaking Polish to their daughter. She said:

'My parents are coming to visit us in a few months' time. I am looking forward to their stay because it will provide a natural setting for speaking Polish. Up till now I have mainly talked in Polish with my daughter, who is now three-and-a-half, and she understands it perfectly well. But since she started playgroup half a year ago, she just wants to speak English. Having the grandparents around will hopefully make it more worthwhile for her to speak some Polish again.'

Another way to ensure that children will practise the other language is to let them stay abroad on their own with their grandparents – or other relatives or friends. The age at which children will feel confident enough to do this will vary a great deal and it also depends on how well they know the people they are visiting. But if hosts and guests all feel comfortable about it, such visits can be a great success all round.

There may even be an added bonus for the parents in that it gives them a chance to go on a holiday elsewhere. It was Magda, who is also Polish and lives in England married to an Englishman, who first mentioned this to me. Her two children are eight and five years old. She said:

'Up till now we have spent almost all our holidays in Poland. But, frankly speaking, I want to see a bit more of the world myself. The plan for this summer is that the children will go to Poland together to stay with my parents. This way they have a chance to see the family and practise their Polish, while there will still be time and money left for us to go elsewhere for our holiday.'

Holidays abroad – or having visitors from abroad – offer a natural opportunity for a language to be used and practised, and I feel it is very important for a child to be able to see some point in learning or keeping up a second language. The fact that more and more parents are now choosing to bring up their children bilingually, and are doing so successfully, may actually have a lot to do with travel being so much easier.

One begins almost to wonder whether parents could in fact leave it to those holiday occasions and forget about the bilingual upbringing at home. The point is, however, that a language can't be learned from scratch within the time limit set by a holiday period. It is true that children can tremendously improve upon their command of a language over a two, three, or four week period, but only if the basic knowledge of the language is there. A parent who was quite explicit on this matter was Angelina. She came from Spain to live in England and marry an Englishman almost twenty years ago. She had the following observation:

'My children have been accepted in Spain as Spanish children, because they can speak the language when they go there. Communication must be given a chance, otherwise people are less interested in you as a person. If we had gone to visit my relatives and friends in Spain with the children just speaking English, they would never have had a chance to become fully integrated in the lifestyle of the people we know there. And because they were accepted and integrated, they learned to speak the language even better.'

A matter of taste

In my search for information on parents and bilingual children I often came across families where one or both parents seemed to have a particular interest in languages. Such an interest may not be a necessary condition for marrying someone from abroad or for moving abroad oneself, but it certainly helps. And for many people it is by no means a mere coincidence that they end up living in a country where the language spoken is the language they studied at university.

Parents with this kind of background and keen on studying languages themselves are usually very enthusiastic about bringing up their children bilingually. But like all other parents they have to adopt a pragmatic standpoint on the matter. These parents had certainly succeeded in doing so: Marie-Luce is French, her husband is English, and they both teach French at a university in the North of England. Both were at home when I arrived to interview them. Marie-Luce:

'When we met we were both fairly fluent in each other's language, but although we have lived in England since our marriage we have mostly communicated in French with each other. When Maxime was born it was fairly natural for both of us to speak French to him, for that was the language of the house. Moreover, we wanted to establish French as a language before he would be exposed to English, which he would learn in any case. Also, we reckoned that if English had been his first language, the need to learn French wouldn't have been half as strong from his point of view. So for Maxime, and for his younger brother, French was the first language.'

Her husband continued:

'Nowadays, however, English is a lot more around in the house, not least because the two boys, now six-and-a-half and four years old, always talk English to each other. I also speak English more regularly, for instance when playing with the boys, as their games become more intricate and technical each day. And we are both convinced that conflict situations are to be avoided, as language development should be natural and we want to be careful not to build up any resentment.'

Language and culture

Language can't be isolated from the rest of life. A nation's language is inextricably linked with its culture and there is no way of separating the two. I found people very aware of this. During almost every interview my informants would sooner or later bring up the relationship between language and other aspects of life. The relationship isn't always simple or straightforward, but parents frequently mentioned the fact that one can't talk about the circumstances of a bilingual upbringing without looking at what it means to live with two cultures as well as two languages.

Françoise comes from France, lives in London, and has an English husband. She simply stated:

'Language is a way of life. It's food, discipline, children's bed-time, the way you spend your free time. My children know both ways: in England they know how to be English children, in France they can be part of the French community.'

An important reason why parents want their children to become bilingual is that they want them to be familiar with the culture of the other country. For people who feel strongly about their background, teaching their children their own language is a way (though it is not the only way) of transmitting their own identity.

Johan's parents moved from Hungary to Australia when he was nine years old. As an adult he moved to England and through his education and training English has inevitably become the language in which he expresses himself most fluently. However, he has always regretted the loss of the Hungarian language and culture by his family in Australia. His wife is also Hungarian and moved from Hungary to England upon their marriage. I spoke to her and she told me:

'We decided that the children should be brought up with both Hungarian and English. For me and my husband Hungarian has always been our main language of communication, although I speak English fairly easily as I worked in a London office for a number of years before our first daughter was born. Both of us have always talked in Hungarian to our daughters, who are now eight and six years old. At the same time, English has gradually taken over as the more important language for the girls through school and social contacts. My husband, however, is quite strict in his efforts to keep up Hungarian, even by practising reading and writing the language with them, something he had to re-learn as an adult.'

The decision to keep up a foreign language is different for couples with a single-language marriage than for parents in a mixed-language marriage. It is easier for parents with a common native tongue to use this with their children than for a parent who is the only one who speaks the other language. But, especially after the children have reached school age, it always needs a certain commitment on behalf of the parents to see to it that their own language and culture are passed on to their children.

Suso and his wife come from Catalonia in Spain and together they have lived in England for fourteen years now. He pointed out that his children, who are now thirteen and ten years old, were not bilingual in Spanish and English, as I first assumed, but in Catalan and English. The Catalan language has been preserved in Spain in spite of many years of oppression and it seems that this couple try to continue the tradition, even far away from their country of origin. I was given the impression that Suso's determination to do so has had the required results so far. But he also insisted that just keeping up the language is not enough, for he said:

'If you want to teach your children your own language, you have to teach them about your culture as well. Some immigrants don't even know their own history and then you cannot expect the children to feel proud of it.'

Changing circumstances

The decision to bring up one's children with two languages is hardly one that can be taken once and for all. Changing circumstances and unexpected reactions from the children may force parents to alter course. Whether parents decide to teach their children two languages simultaneously, whether they put them through the process of learning a second language after the first has been established, or whether they want to keep up the first language after the children have acquired a second one, parents have to opt for a bilingual upbringing time and again. And it always needs an effort on the part of the parents to see to it that their children become or remain bilingual.

Jeanette moved from Holland to marry an Englishman when her children were nine, ten, and twelve years old. Her story:

'My first concern was that the children would learn English and I actually started teaching them while we were still living in Holland. We sat down for an English lesson twice a week and I even gave them some homework to do. Before we moved to England, we spent a short holiday there, but at that time the children were quite disappointed when they found out how little they already knew of the language. After we had settled, however, and they had started school, English came along fairly quickly, especially for the boy, who is the youngest of the three. They have all received remedial teaching at school and from the beginning we made an effort to speak English at home during mealtimes.

'And now, after three years the problem has reversed 180 degrees. My main concern now is to keep up Dutch, and it is turning out to be more difficult than I had anticipated. I would have thought that my children had reached an age where a language is so well established that they wouldn't forget it. But this is true only if you really make an effort to keep it up. Also, we live in the North of England and we have to make quite an effort to go to Holland. For this reason the children don't get as much practice as I would like them to have.'

Jeanette's case isn't all that extraordinary. Circumstances may change more quickly and more drastically than we sometimes like to think. She is not the only mother I talked to who moved abroad with her children to marry again. For younger children the transition might be easier, but it is true that children don't necessarily learn a new language quite naturally or automatically. And keeping up an old one is even less automatic, for the language spoken at school will gradually take over as the more important one for the children.

At any given time, life may force us into a sudden change of direction. What happens after a divorce, or when one of the parents dies, and the surviving parent considers returning to his or her country of origin? None of the parents I talked to actually mentioned the possibility of becoming a single parent – and therefore of wanting or needing to return to the country of origin – as a reason for bringing up their children with two languages. After all, we can't predict or guard ourselves against all possible events in life. But the eventuality of going back to one's own country can be in the back of one's mind. Many considerations will come to bear upon such a decision, and language will only be one of them. Let us see what the reality looked like for someone who had to face this situation.

Mushi moved from England to live in Paris fourteen years ago when she married a Frenchman. They separated five years ago when the children were seven, three, and two. She explained her situation to me:

'I considered going back to England, but it turned out to be impossible for me to find either a job or suitable housing there. Here I can at least earn some kind of living by teaching English as a foreign language. The children understand English and I will sometimes speak it with them, for one consequence of the separation has been that I myself speak a lot more English and far less French than when I was still married. But my children are basically French children. When they were born I decided they should become firmly rooted in one country, for I never had that experience myself. It is important to me that my children should feel at home here, even if for myself I have given up hope of becoming fully integrated into the French way of life.'

Advantages

So far I have suggested a number of reasons and circumstances which affect how parents decide upon a bilingual upbringing for their children. Up till now, it seems as if the reasons that were mentioned were all at least as much for the parents' sake as for the children's. It won't come as a surprise, though, that parents who are in favour of having more than one language around usually also produce a long list of the advantages this has for the children.

When asked about the advantages of a bilingual upbringing, one father simply wrote down 'legion'. Others were more specific, and the answers given most regularly were: 'knowing two languages makes it easier to learn a third or fourth', 'later it will benefit them job-wise', 'increases self-confidence', 'makes them more tolerant and open-minded', and 'more choices and more chances'. And Anne, who brought up two children in France while she and her husband both have English as their mother tongue, wrote:

'The obvious advantages are that two worlds are open to you rather than only one. Besides being able to communicate verbally with everyone, from the dustman to the distinguished neighbours, the mentality of the people of a particular country becomes familiar to you through language. Therefore, later on, in the working world for example, you are not only able to converse but also able to understand and cope with people.'

Only one parent I talked to was somewhat more cynical when asked about the advantages of a bilingual upbringing for the children themselves. She remarked:

'I used to study languages and it is true that people with a bilingual background were often streets ahead of the rest of us. No doubt it is very useful if you want to become a simultaneous translator. But how many of our children will actually choose that as a profession?'

Parents can go on discussing endlessly the advantages, and disadvantages, of a bilingual upbringing but there is a distinct lack of real information to go on. So I talked to some teenagers who have come through the bilingual experience and are probably in the best position to talk about the costs and benefits. Their views are expressed in Chapter 8. And in the very next chapter some of the disadvantages will be spelled out by those parents who had their own reasons for not pressing ahead with a bilingual upbringing for their children.

4

Deciding against a bilingual upbringing

When I phoned people and asked if I could interview them about their experience of bringing up their children in a bilingual home environment, the answer would sometimes be: 'Yes, but my children are not bilingual.' I would then explain that I was not only interested in the 'success stories', but in all the experiences of the parents concerned, whether or not they had brought up their children with two languages. It subsequently appeared that people were very willing to talk about their reasons for not going through with a bilingual upbringing for their offspring. So before we discuss how children can become bilingual, let us first have a look at how and why some parents have decided against a bilingual upbringing.

How do parents choose what is important when bringing up children? Well, they all have different childhood memories, they all reach parenthood via many different routes and for many different reasons, and they all expect different things from life. All these things influence the way parents raise their children, and the bilingual upbringing is only one of the many aspects about which parents have to make up their minds. By looking at some of the decisions against a bilingual upbringing and trying to find out more about the reasons behind those decisions, I feel new parents will then be able to make an informed and responsible choice.

Options

When I arrived to do the interview, Ingrid and John were both present. For a whole evening we sat and discussed the pros and cons of a bilingual upbringing. Occasionally, the conversation took another direction as we talked about my beloved Amsterdam, where they had lived for a couple of years in the same part of town where I grew up. But I was there to hear about bilingual children and their parents' experiences, and by the time I left I had learned a lot. I also knew more than ever before that no two interviews on this subject would be the same.

John is English, and comes from a bilingual English–French background. He studied linguistics at university, but he no longer works in that field. Ingrid is Norwegian and was brought up in Norway. They met in Switzerland while they were both working and studying there but they have lived in England for most of their married life. They like learning different languages, as is illustrated by the fact that the two of them learned to speak Dutch when they lived in Holland.

All this so far is fairly typical of a couple in a mixed-language marriage. What makes these people less typical is that – notwithstanding their own interest in and talent for languages – they decided against a bilingual upbringing for their children. Ingrid began:

'When my oldest was born, I actually did talk Norwegian to him, as we were living in France at the time and we didn't have that much English around anyway. But we came to England when he was eighteen months old and from then onwards I have only spoken English to him and his younger brother.'

John continued:

'I am against a bilingual upbringing in principle, as I think that communication is difficult enough as it is and it implies taking risks with a young mind. I have seen adverse results in the past and I don't want the children to get confused. I have a background in linguistics myself and I believe that learning different languages is a talent. For those who have such a talent, it can always be developed at a later age.'

Ingrid then added:

'I love English as a language and it felt silly at the time to be the only one around to speak Norwegian to the child. Moreover, who needs Norwegian as a language?'

Their two sons are now teenagers. According to the parents, the elder of the two, if not bilingual English–Norwegian, certainly has developed a flair for languages and finds speaking new languages easy, although he doesn't like studying them the academic way. And in spite of the fact that the children went to English-speaking schools while the family lived in Holland, he still picked up some Dutch, if only through watching television. As far as the younger one is concerned, the parents are convinced that English is the only language he will ever like and need.

A bilingual background

Not all the people I talked to were as articulate in their opinions as Ingrid and John, but most of them were very definite as to why they hadn't brought up their children with two languages. It may come as a surprise, but among the parents who decided against a bilingual upbringing were quite a few who came from a bilingual background themselves. One of them was Janine. She comes from the French-speaking part of Belgium, but she spent her childhood in several different countries. She met her English husband in Brussels eight years ago, but soon afterwards they moved to London together, where all their four children were born. She told me her reasons for not speaking French with her children:

'English comes very naturally to me. Although French is the language I have been brought up with, English has been part of my life for a long time. I lived in Cyprus when I was a teenager and went to an English-speaking secondary school there. John was learning French when we met and he speaks it reasonably well, but our common language has always been English, even in French-speaking surroundings. I would feel like a stranger in my own house if I spoke French to my children. Eventually I would like my children to speak French, but only time will tell whether I will regret that I didn't bring them up with two languages from the very beginning.'

A substantial number of the parents I talked to were the offspring of a mixed-language marriage themselves or they had moved abroad with their parents when they were young. How does the first-hand experience of having been brought up with two languages influence the decision for one's own children? I found two distinct patterns. Among parents who come from a bilingual background, some are particularly proud to continue the tradition of a bilingual upbringing and make a conscious decision to do so, as we saw in the previous chapter. Others, however, don't want to repeat the experience of a bilingual home environment with their own children, as they have come to feel so at home in their new language that it would be rather artificial for them to switch back to their original mother tongue.

Mieke was twenty-one when she migrated from Holland to Australia with her parents and younger brothers and sisters. Six years later she married an Englishman and settled in England. She said:

'I had adopted an English way of life, including the language, before I had children. I never really considered teaching my children Dutch and they have never shown much interest at all. I thought it was more important for them to learn good English and it also seemed to me that Dutch wasn't a very useful language to know.'

The utility principle

The usefulness of a language, also referred to as the 'utility principle', has now been mentioned a couple of times. So let's talk a bit more about this 'utility principle', as it crops up in almost any conversation about bilingualism.

Is it possible to say that one language is more useful than another? English functions as a means of communication for many different people all over the world and one could indeed say that it is a more useful language than one that is spoken by only a small number of people. French is also thought of as a very useful language to know and the effect of this is that to bring up one's children to become bilingual English–French is usually thought of rather positively. But in cases where Danish or Dutch are being kept up by the parents it is often considered to be nothing but an extra burden on the child to have to learn such a language.

Dutch people themselves often point out that their language is not very useful and, generally speaking, they do not stand up for their own language. As we have seen in Chapter 2, Dutch native speakers are usually quite proud of their ability to speak foreign languages and they find it difficult to think of a reason why anyone would want to learn their language. Similarly, Dutch people who live abroad are often not strongly motivated to keep up the language with their children.

One of them is Marian, who comes from Holland and lives in the south of France with Georges, who is French. We know each other from the time when we were both students together in Amsterdam and she is one of the parents to whom I sent a questionnaire. She wrote:

'When Georges and I first met twelve years ago our language of communication was English. Upon settling in France together, our common language soon became French. Our three boys, now seven, five, and three years old, were all born in France and we both have always talked French to them. Sometimes I wonder: "Is it through laziness or lack of discipline that I never even tried teaching them Dutch?" It was by far the easiest thing to do to bring them up with just French. Moreover, who needs Dutch other than the people who actually live in Holland? Also, the house is often full of people who speak many different languages, so the children are used to hearing the various sounds. I just hope when they start learning other languages at school that because of this they will get the idea pretty quickly.'

We have to remember, though, that the practical usefulness of a language is not the only criterion that determines whether it is preserved by its native speakers. It is people's attitude towards their own language more than anything else that decides whether a language continues to be used, and a great number of languages spoken by only very few people are known to have survived in many places in the world, at many points in history, and for many different reasons. However, the study of minority languages – and the reasons behind the loss or preservation of languages – is a subject in its own right, and as

29

this book describes individual families, rather than overall trends or theories, it's a subject that falls outside its scope.

Firmly rooted

A common characteristic of bilingual families is that at least one of the parents doesn't live in his or her country of origin. For some people, moving abroad is a once-in-a-lifetime event. Others develop a taste for it and travel around quite a bit before deciding to settle. The latter group of people may have accepted or may even be pleased with the fact that they don't have strong roots. But when they become parents they may still find it important that their children are firmly rooted in one particular place and in one particular language.

Lotte comes from Denmark and she is a sister of one of the other parents I interviewed. She lives with her English husband in a small university town in the North of England and they invited me to go and stay so that I could interview them and a number of other bilingual parents they knew. Lotte told me:

'I was brought up in a middle-class family in a large European city and came to England when I was twenty. My husband is English, but he lived in Holland and Germany during part of his childhood. Neither of us has a strong emotional attachment to any particular place of dwelling. But our children are born and raised in a small northern English town, which I think must have an effect on their outlook on life. Even if they never return here in later life, they will feel they have their roots in a very particular spot and nowhere else.

'The children are not bilingual, but as we regularly have foreign guests and travel abroad with the whole family, I know they are familiar with different languages and different cultures. I think it is more important to bring up your children with tolerance and respect for other ways of living than for them to be fluent in another language.'

An interesting thing about this family is that Lotte's husband is a lecturer in Italian and most holidays abroad are therefore spent in Italy. If the children are familiar with another language, it is Italian rather than Danish! During my stay with them my impression was that these parents were certainly trying to bring up their children with minds open to other people, other languages, and other cultures, but that the Danish language and culture were not made to figure very prominently.

A similar reason for not bringing up the children with two languages, at least not from the earliest moment onwards, was given by Christine, as she also considered it to be very important for her children to become firmly rooted in one language. Christine is English, but she lives in

Holland and is married to a Dutchman. She spoke mainly Dutch to her children, who are now eight and five years old, until they started going to school. Christine's decision is particularly noteworthy, for one would not really expect an English parent to give up speaking English with the children, especially if the other language is usually considered to be a rather less useful one. But she wrote to me:

'When the children were small, I felt that the most important factor was for children to have a mother tongue and to be emotionally based in the language of their homeland and culture. I thought it was more important to master one language 100 per cent than two languages 90 per cent. The social and emotional tie with the 100 per cent language was to be weighed against the risk of feeling in a no-man's land with two: neither belonging wholly here nor wholly there.'

However, she also added:

'Latterly I have changed my mind and attach less weight to this point of view.'

It seems that she is now more confident that the two languages can coexist and therefore is speaking English with her children more often. And in fact the evidence collected during my interviewing suggests that two languages can and do happily coexist in many bilingual households.

Postponing

Of course, yet another possibility for parents is to postpone the decision on a bilingual upbringing till some later date. For if parents decide against a bilingual upbringing when the children are young, it doesn't necessarily mean that they oppose all bilingual experience later on. Rather, they want to wait until the children are somewhat older so that a better assessment of the children's abilities can be made. Also, some parents feel that the children's own opinion should have some weight and that it is up to the children themselves to express the need for getting to know another language.

Mary is English and has lived in France since her marriage to a Frenchman fourteen years ago. Their house is in a small village north of Paris. She had the following story to tell:

'When my oldest son was born, I knew I was going back to work and that a French woman would be looking after him. For that reason it didn't seem right to start speaking English to him from the very beginning. When he was eighteen months old, I stopped working and I thought maybe now is the time to start with English. But the baby still didn't talk at all, so I felt he needed encouragement in one language

31

rather than being confused with a second one. As it turned out, he didn't start to talk until he was three, and later he also had some problems at school.

'Looking back I know that an extra language would have been too much of a burden for this child and I am glad I never persisted. Now that he is eight, he has English classes at school. I think he likes them, because his friends are also learning English and now his own background gives him a bit of an upper hand.'

To give the children a fair chance to express their own needs rather than to force anything upon them, was one of the reasons put forward by this next father for not talking Dutch to his children when they were small. He is Dutch and his wife is English and they have always lived in England. As we will see in Chapter 10, which focusses on the role of fathers, it is fairly difficult in any case to keep up the father's language if he is the only parent who comes from abroad. But this father also had the following considerations:

'I want my two boys to find out for themselves about possible advantages and disadvantages. So far they haven't been to Holland that often, but last year they stayed there on their own for a while, and probably this will happen more often as they get older. If they decide they want to learn Dutch after all, I will of course give them my support.'

The problem is of course that – whatever parents decide with respect to the bilingual upbringing – the children's future is being decided for them. As they grow older, children may make choices themselves, but such choices will always be based upon what they already did or did not learn from their parents. Monolingual children (of bilingual parents) may gradually discover for themselves the advantages or disadvantages of knowing only one language, but learning a second language at a later age is never the same as being brought up with two languages from the very beginning.

Giving up

Living with two languages will affect children in many ways and some of the effects may not always be positive. But I think that problems will usually not be caused by a bilingual setting *per se*, but rather by a whole set of circumstances, and it all very much depends on how an individual child reacts to a certain situation.

Some parents told me that, because of various problems, they had stopped speaking their own language with their children, and thus had given up on the bilingual upbringing. But usually this had happened when the children were still quite young and before conflict situations had had a chance to grow out of hand. An example of this was offered by Ulla. She lives in London, but comes from Germany. She met her first English husband while living in Switzerland. She remembered:

'The older boy was born in England, but soon afterwards we moved back to Switzerland and we stayed there for another two years. During that period, there were lots of different languages around all the time. On our return to England, I felt the child had been messed around enough. We all needed a break and sticking to one language only was an important part of that. By the time my second boy was born, English was so firmly established as the language of the house that the question of speaking German to my children was never really raised again.'

Strictly speaking, giving up on a bilingual upbringing is not the same as deciding against it from the very beginning. But on more than one occasion I noticed that the arguments parents would put forward against a bilingual upbringing had only been formulated by them after they had actually given up. In fact, giving up on a bilingual upbringing is a reality that many parents may face at some point during the bilingual upbringing. We will come back to this issue in Chapter 9, The Role of Mothers, where some more reasons why parents give up will be discussed.

Disadvantages

In describing why parents decide against a bilingual upbringing, I have mentioned a number of the possible disadvantages: it is taking an unknown risk; by making them learn a less useful language, parents are putting an extra burden on a child; by not having one mother tongue, a child doesn't acquire firm emotional ties with a language or culture; children should be allowed their own choice.

Not surprisingly, parents who decided against having two languages for their children were usually more specific in spelling out the disadvantages. During my conversations with them, some people actually started telling 'horror stories': cases of bilingual children who ended up being quite disturbed, who had problems with stuttering, who were severely behind at school. However, in my search for material I did not go by hearsay information and I myself have not come across any children with serious problems resulting from their bilingual home environment.

On the whole, the arguments against a bilingual upbringing seem to me somewhat less convincing than the arguments in favour. Children have an innate ability for learning and growing and I have come to believe that through a bilingual upbringing each child's potential – rather than being restricted or overburdened – can be developed even more. However, there is no rule that tells parents whether they should opt for a bilingual upbringing or decide against it, and parents should feel free to make their own decision.

5
Becoming bilingual – the children

Until now we have been mainly looking at the bilingual experience from the parents' point of view – discussing their options, their problems, and their dilemmas. But whatever choice parents make, or whatever strategy they adopt, each child will react very specifically to the situation, and the way a child reacts will determine the final outcome more than anything else. Parents who are aware of the different possible reactions of their children have a greater chance of succeeding in bringing them up bilingually. So from this point on I shall be paying as much attention to the reactions of the children as to the reasons why parents take a certain course of action.

New parents who have decided on a bilingual upbringing often wonder whether one way of going about it is better than another and they may be looking for guidance on how to proceed. So in this chapter we shall take a look at the various strategies that parents can adopt to make learning easier for the children in a bilingual household, and in the following three chapters we shall follow the children's actual development in a bilingual home environment from when they are tiny toddlers until they are conscious and critical teenagers.

Before going on to describe a number of possible strategies, I want to emphasize that there is not really one 'best' way of proceeding with a bilingual upbringing. What is the right way for one family may not work for another. Also, I think that most parents who are in a bilingual situation have a 'gut feeling' about what they would like to do with respect to the bilingual upbringing of their children and how they would like to do it. I firmly believe that parents should trust their own feelings and judgements – and share them with other parents – and not let 'experts' tell them whether these feelings are 'right' or what the 'best' method would be.

Strategies

One strategy that parents can adopt is the one-person-one-language method. This is where one parent speaks one language with the child, and the other parent another language. It is a strategy most commonly applied by parents in a mixed-language marriage. Indeed, if the partner whose native tongue is the local language doesn't speak the language of the partner who comes from abroad, it is the only possible way to proceed. An example would be a French mother and an English father (who doesn't speak French) who live in England and who want their children to be able to speak both French and English.

A second strategy is to use one language (the foreign language) in the home and the other language (the language spoken locally) outside the home. This is the strategy usually adopted by parents with a single-language marriage. For them it usually feels most natural to communicate within the family in the original mother tongue, and then to use the local language for all contacts outside the home. This method can also be applied by parents with a mixed-language marriage in cases where both partners are reasonably fluent in each other's language.

If either of these two strategies is used, then the child learns two languages at the same time, which is known as 'simultaneous acquisition'. According to a third strategy a child learns the second language after learning the first, otherwise known as 'successive acquisition'. Only one language is used with the child up till a certain age and then the other language is introduced (between age three and five, for instance).

A fourth strategy is to adopt no particular strategy at all and to use the two languages whenever and wherever it is most convenient: factors such as time, topic, person, and place decide which language is spoken. In a way this 'strategy' is being used by almost all parents some of the time. For, even if parents choose one of the first three, it is practically impossible to be consistent at all times in all situations. If you are able to switch languages, then you find that in daily life you are constantly required to do this.

On the following pages a number of families describe how they have applied these strategies and how successful, or not so successful, they were in doing so.

The one-person-one-language method

Among the parents I talked to, there were two who told me that they had sought professional advice on how to bring up their children with two languages. One mother said she had talked to a child psychiatrist about it, the other to a paediatrician. The advice both experts had come up with was to keep the two languages strictly separate: the one-person-one-language method.

This is the strategy described in many academic case studies of bilingual children and it is the one that child-care experts tend to feel that they can recommend. And certainly, in mixed-language marriages where only the partner from abroad is bilingual and the 'local' parent doesn't speak the foreign language, it does seem the only way to establish a pattern in the bilingual language development of the child.

One parent who has been using this strategy is Simone. She is French and has been living in England for eleven years. She is married to an Englishman and she describes his knowledge of French as 'very limited'. Their little daughter is almost three. She wrote this about their experiences as a family living in the South of England:

'I speak only French to her and her father speaks in English. She started nursery school at two-and-a-half, because I felt that her English was not developing as quickly as her French. I am with her every day and there are some situations she has not experienced in English – for example going to the swimming pool, taking a plane, etc.

'We still speak to her as before, but I have already noticed that she shows more interest in English, for example she asks what her father is saying, or how he says certain words, often while looking at pictures in a book. When our daughter reaches a comparable level in both languages, I think I might limit her French to mealtimes and when she is with me only, although it is too early yet to make a decision on this.'

Another parent who wrote about her experiences with this strategy was Joëlle. She comes from Switzerland and French is her mother tongue. She has lived in England for almost twenty years, married to an Englishman. They have two teenagers. She wrote that she and her husband have always spoken English together, even though he speaks excellent French. They made a conscious decision to bring up the children bilingually and chose the one-person-one-language strategy:

'With Olivia I spoke French and my husband spoke English. She spoke very well by the time she was eighteen months–two years, always addressing me in French and her father in English.'

She then continues:

'However, things gradually changed because my son refused right from the start to speak any French at all. I spoke French with my daughter and son till they were about five and two-and-a-half respectively. Then my son started kindergarten and he would not even really answer me if I spoke French – but we went on for about a year longer.

'We decided when our son was about three-and-a-half that it was more important for him to talk and master one language rather than mess around. I found it too much of a strain to deal with both children in different languages so we went over to speaking English.'

It is clear that there are some problems with this strategy. Does one really want to keep the two languages strictly apart for different roles, even if those roles are so closely linked together, such as being a spouse and being a parent? One obvious result is that one of the parties involved may feel left out. Joëlle:

'We both think that one of the probable reasons our son wouldn't speak French was that my husband and I always spoke English together and he felt excluded from our "intimate relationship" language.'

The problem is not always between parents and child. If the marriage is going through a difficult patch, then the bilingual situation can make the problems between husband and wife worse. As one mother put it, the situation of speaking one language with the children from which the spouse is excluded may lead to the 'creating of a secret society in one's own house'.

Inside and outside the house

The next strategy, to use one language inside the house and the other one for outside contacts, is generally easier to maintain and it is the natural one to be adopted by parents with a single-language marriage. And by applying this strategy one particular problem can be avoided: there is no chance of someone feeling left out. For this reason it also makes sense for parents in a mixed-language marriage where both partners speak the foreign language to use only that language in the house.

However, one other problem may arise, namely that the children may find it difficult to learn the local language, and therefore may have a much more difficult time adapting when they start going to school. For this reason, parents who apply the 'inside–outside' strategy often wonder whether they only need to teach their children their mother tongue or whether it is also up to them to introduce the language spoken locally.

❝ Once we had decided to keep up Dutch with the children, this was to be our only language of communication at home, while they would have to learn English at playgroup and through socializing. For a while this seemed to work, except that the children picked up English very slowly. One day, however, Gideon declared that he wanted to practise his English at home. As by that time he had kept his mouth shut at playgroup for more than six months we reluctantly gave in, thinking that it might give a boost to his confidence.

Bathtime was chosen as the English conversation hour and on the very first occasion Gideon did actually start to chat in English. Obviously, he had already acquired some command of the language but had been waiting for the right time and place to practise it. But, whether or not it was beneficial for his confidence, it soon ruined mine. For a child's world contains umpteen interesting objects and activities whose English name I did not happen to know: soap-dish, all sorts of bath animals, jumping on one foot, to mention just a few. Moreover, lots of objects or areas in the house have acquired a sort of proper name in Dutch, such as "pappamammaskamer" for our bedroom. From the start I was mixing English and Dutch to an extent that I had never thought possible. After a short time we abandoned the English conversation hour and reinstated the Dutch-only strategy. **9**

In families where only one language is spoken at home, while the other language is reserved for contacts outside, the children usually achieve a reasonable fluency in the home language before they begin to acquire some fluency in the 'outside' language. The development in the two languages will usually overlap to some extent, however, and this brings us to the next issue.

Successive or simultaneous acquisition?

The point is often raised whether children should learn two languages at the same time or one after the other. In practice, there is often not much choice in this matter. When a family moves from one country to another with children who have already acquired one language, the job of learning a second one quite clearly comes after they have already acquired a first language.

But parents whose children are born after migration, or parents with a mixed-language marriage often wonder whether one way is better than the other. Should a child have a firm basis in one language before the second one is introduced, or can a child deal with learning two languages at the same time from the very beginning? Several parents offered their opinions on this matter, while describing their own experiences with doing it one way or the other. One of them was Kerstin, a Swedish mother of two little daughters who were brought up with English and Swedish from the start. She wrote:

'I think it is not more difficult to learn two than to learn one language from the start. As babies have to acquire a language anyway, there is no reason for them to believe that an object, for example, has only one name.

'The older one very confidently switches between the two languages and seems to feel equally at home in both, although she sometimes uses English words, puts Swedish endings on them, and puts them into Swedish sentences. The younger one doesn't talk yet, but understands both languages very well indeed.'

But Simone, the mother who wrote about her experience with the one-person-one-language method, also reported:

'It is more work for the parents who have to make a conscious decision of speaking the one language, whenever and wherever, and it is certainly more work for the child who has to learn twice as much as another child.'

The fear of confusing the child if he or she is confronted with two languages from the start is also quite frequently mentioned by parents. But even if the foreign language is used exclusively at home, the local language always plays some role in the child's life, through contacts with the outside world. The only way to create a situation where the child really learns one language after the other – the successive acquisition strategy – is to begin by speaking the local language at home and to introduce the foreign language at a later age.

In a way it seems a rather unlikely situation for parents who have a common foreign mother tongue to speak the local language with the children. But those who want their children to integrate as much and as quickly as possible may do just that. However, the consequence often is that the children do not learn the foreign language at all.

For parents in a mixed-language marriage the situation is different, especially if they have always spoken the local language to each other. If they feel uncomfortable about the one-person-one-language approach, the choice can be made to adopt the 'successive acquisition' strategy and to start off with the local language, while the foreign one is introduced at a later age. This situation was described by Anna Maria. She is Italian and is married to an Englishman. As he doesn't speak any Italian, they have always used English together. They have one eight-year-old daughter. Anna Maria wrote:

'I had conflicting thoughts about teaching a baby two languages at the same time. I thought it might be confusing for the child at a particular stage in life before having acquired certain rooted structures. Because my Italian at the time had lost its fluency and the baby would have been in touch with an English community first before an Italian one, the choice to speak English to her was made on those bases.

'At the age of four my daughter was presented with the Italian language and she has been learning it since then – so she is now taught in Italian, but we still carry on talking to her in English at home. She can now read, write, speak, understand, and think in either language.'

In the case of successive acquisition, a child more often seems to be taught the language more or less formally, rather than picking it up 'naturally'. In mixed-language marriages where the father is the 'foreign' parent, this strategy appears to be particularly appropriate and we will come across some examples of this in Chapter 10.

Switching languages

Parents who are involved in a bilingual upbringing are bilingual themselves and this means that children hear their parents speaking different languages to different people. If, then, a parent uses only one particular language for communicating with the child, the child still knows that this doesn't reflect the parent's way of communication in general.

The fourth strategy – to use no strategy at all and to speak either language whenever and wherever it is most convenient – doesn't seem very suitable in the initial stages of a bilingual upbringing. But parents who use one of the other three strategies often report that a child at some point refuses to speak the foreign language, the language that has been exclusively used for contact between parent and child. One of the reasons for this may well be that if the parent is seen, or rather heard, by a child to switch languages the child wants to do the same thing.

The example a parent is offering a child can also have a positive effect. As an answer to my question whether she would describe her child as being or becoming bilingual, Simone wrote:

'It is rather early to say, but what is sure is that she is completely fluent in French while living in England. She does not seem to mind speaking two languages – indeed she hears me speaking both, depending to whom I am speaking. As things stand now, I would think she has every chance of becoming bilingual.'

It is often said that the various strategies only work if parents are really strict about keeping the languages separate. I think better advice to parents would be for them to be flexible, for only then can children learn what it means to be bilingual: to be able to switch languages according to needs and circumstances.

Rules

One question I asked the parents was whether they had any specific rules for dealing with the bilingual situation at home. It seemed to me that this was the sort of thing that would be interesting and helpful for new parents, or for those who are faced with a particular problem. But the answers turned out to be different from what I expected.

Only a few parents told me that they had any specific rules. One of them was Angelina, a Spanish mother who lives in London. When we talked about how parents can provide enough stimulating material in both languages – in this case reading material – she told me:

'My way of making it attractive for them to read in Spanish has been to buy Spanish cartoons. I don't allow English cartoons in the house, so you could say I have bribed them into reading Spanish, for otherwise they would probably have seen no use in doing so.'

Generally, though, parents who tried to create some kind of regulations often encountered some unexpected consequences. The problem with rules is that children have unique ways of drawing up their own principles that are bound to counteract their parents' intentions. It was Janine who told me the following story:

'"Now that you are in France, you must speak French", Rachel's grandmother had said when we were there on a holiday. My daughter actually made an effort but, the next time grandmama came to visit us in England and I had hoped for a follow-up of the French lesson, Rachel decided: "Now that you are in England, you must speak English to me."'

The one rule that was mentioned frequently was this: out of politeness, parents will not speak the foreign language in the company of children or adults who would not be able to understand it, especially at home or when being invited to someone else's house. One of the first times that we tried to apply this rule at home the following thing happened:

❬ After we had been living in London for eighteen months and Gideon was just starting to express himself in English at playgroup, we invited one of his playmates over for lunch. Our Dutch au-pair asked the little boy what kind of sandwich he would like and then posed the same question to Gideon, also addressing him in English. Gideon burst into tears and cried (in Dutch): "Scot is English so you speak to him in English. But I am Dutch, so you must speak to me in Dutch." ❭

The bilingual development

One mother noted about her children:

'To be bilingual still means for them that their command of the one language is better than that of the other, while even their best language is never quite as good as it would have been if they had had to know only one language. So it always seems a matter of gaining on the one hand and losing on the other.'

Whatever strategy or rules are being applied, it is almost always the case that, at any one time, the child is more fluent in one language than in the other. The respective languages spoken by the child will each feature as the more important or 'dominant' language in different stages of the child's bilingual development. Whether both languages are spoken at home from the beginning or whether it is only the foreign language, the language spoken at school will gradually take over for most or all purposes. The use of the foreign language may even disappear altogether for a shorter or longer period of time. We may see this happen in particular with children of primary school age, and we shall talk about this again in Chapter 7.

The important thing to remember is that bilingualism for a child is not the same as bilingualism for an adult. First of all, for a child bilingualism is even more of a process than it is for an adult, and in relation to children we should therefore always talk about becoming rather than being bilingual.

Secondly, there is a difference in degree of proficiency. When saying that a child knows two languages, one means to indicate that she or he has a certain fluency in those languages in accordance with her or his age. A child doesn't have the same command of a language as an adult. By age five a child will have acquired most basic language skills, but there remains a lot to be learned with respect to vocabulary and more complex sentence structures, whether a child is learning one or two languages.

Cécile, who is French and lives in Oxford, England, with an English husband, gave the following description of the bilingual development of her two sons, who are now seven and three-and-a-half years old:

'My older son learned French first; but when he went to playgroup at two-and-a-half he became very fluent (and better) in English. During that period we also stayed five months in Spain where he went to a nursery school – he learned a lot of Spanish but forgot it within four months of coming back.

'Since going to nursery and primary school, English is the dominant language, the one he can use with all the "nuances", subtleties, etc... His spoken French is more basic – he could not really have a proper conversation with an adult in French for instance.

'My younger son, who is now three-and-a-half, started to speak English when he was two-and-a-half; he now seems to know the French equivalent for the most basic words – but his sentences tend to be in English. And with both of them, they will answer in English even if we speak to them in French.'

Another important point to realize is that the different languages being learned during the bilingual development will have an influence on each other, also referred to as 'interference'. Parents are often aware of this interference, as shown in the following account. Elisabeth and her husband are both English. The elder of their two boys is now almost six years old. The family have lived in Holland since before he was born. She wrote:

'Vocabulary is probably more limited in each language than it would be if only one was spoken. English words are used in Dutch sentences and vice versa, also word order mistakes occur quite often, expressions are literally translated and used in the other language, which can give a rather untidy effect.'

The influence of one language upon the other and the actual mixing of the two languages are sometimes regarded as the more worrying aspects of a bilingual development. The fear of children getting confused appears to be related to the fact that bilingual children often seem to be mixing the two languages.

However, even in adult bilingualism it is unavoidable that some degree of interference between the two languages occurs. But I also think that parents can help children to reduce some of the mixing that takes place. They can point out some of the differences between the two languages – for instance by playing games, such as 'Who will guess the French for ...?' – and they can gently correct their children's language use. Most importantly though, as the children get older and develop their linguistic skills, a lot of the interference will disappear of its own accord.

Temperaments and talents

At some of the interviews I did, parents would begin or end the conversation by commenting that of course it all depended on the children themselves. They would remark that children have different temperaments and talents, and that some of them thrive in a situation where others feel quite bewildered. As Joëlle put it:

'Olivia liked it and Benedict didn't! But I think that temperamentally they are very different anyway – Olivia is an extrovert and Benedict an introvert.'

Not all parents realize to what extent their children's characters may influence the course of events. When parents abandon the attempt to bring their children up bilingually, they may feel that they themselves are to blame for not being consistent enough or for not dealing well with some of the difficulties. They are not helped by those parents who, successful in bringing up their own children with two languages, believe that the procedure that has worked for them will work for others too.

Until quite recently, children from a bilingual background were often perceived as having a handicap. And if these children didn't do well at school, their bilingualism was seen as the cause of their failure. Nowadays, however, it is assumed that children with average intelligence will be able to cope with a bilingual upbringing and will even benefit from it in other learning situations.

But intelligence alone cannot explain children's reactions to bilingualism. Children have an innate ability for learning language, but those with a talent for language – especially for its communicative and creative aspects – will learn a second or third one more easily than others. Some children, for instance, seem to have 'an ear' for different languages and pick them up effortlessly, but other children may have a much harder time before they can express themselves adequately.

The difficulty is that parents, at the time when they opt for a bilingual upbringing, often don't yet know their children's temperaments or talents. This is true for those who decide to create a bilingual home environment for their children from birth onwards and it is also true for couples who move abroad with young children. But as the children grow older parents gain a lot of first-hand experience and recognize that individual children have different talents and react in different ways to similar situations. Parents should therefore always try to choose a course of action that best suits their own and their children's needs.

6
From the beginning – 0–4 year olds

❝A little while after my son Gideon had started primary school, a month or so before his fifth birthday, his English finally seemed to have become more fluent. Then, one day, he came out of school and told me, in Dutch: "Now I have spoken English all day at school, and I didn't even notice." He himself seemed rather pleasantly surprised about the new situation and his remark showed, in retrospect, how conscious and self-conscious he had always been about his limited ability of speaking English. ❞

It made me realize that I was not the only person who had been closely observing the bilingual development of my two children: they themselves have often asked questions or made comments that show how conscious they are of the bilingual situation in which they live. The present chapter is entirely devoted to the reactions of small children and I don't need to remind parents that toddlers have a mind of their own and a strong one too. On the following pages it will become clear that for both parents and children the early stage of a bilingual development is hardly ever an experience that passes by unnoticed.

Theory and practice

I asked my informants: 'Would you agree that the opinion held by the "general public" is that learning a second language comes quickly and easily for young children?' 'Yes', was the answer of by far the majority of the parents I talked to. 'Do you agree with that opinion yourself?' This time many parents said 'no', though a number of them actually did agree and also answered 'yes'.

These two questions and the answers given tell us something about the theory and practice of bringing up young children with two languages: most people think that a bilingual upbringing is just a matter of course, but only parents who have tried know what it takes to make your children bilingual.

A number of preconceived ideas exist as to how young children cope with learning more than one language, and as these notions influence the expectations and thoughts of new parents it is important to have a look at them and set them against reality as experienced by the parents I talked to. Wonder, surprise, and disappointment will be some of the emotions felt by parents in their efforts to bring up their children in a bilingual home environment. Perhaps the only way to avoid disappointment when the children react differently from what was expected or predicted is to look rather more cynically on those predictions or expectations.

Quick and easy

It is generally thought that learning a second language is a quick and easy process for a young child, but many parents who have been through the process with their children tend to disagree. They have watched their children's frustration at not being able to express themselves properly, or they have been through prolonged periods of a child keeping its mouth shut outside the house.

Veronica and her husband are both English. They moved to France six years ago when their two boys were two years and a couple of weeks old. She told me:

'If someone had told me at the time that it would take my older son three years to learn French, I would not have believed it. But that is what it took. The first year Chris learned hardly any French, for he stayed at home with me. He was just beginning to talk in any case and I remember that one of the things he would say was "French fright", which wasn't a very encouraging sign.

'The second year he started attending a local nursery school. During that year he still spoke hardly any French and his frustration regularly made him resort to aggressive behaviour. Only during his second year at the nursery, our third year in France, did he gradually start to understand the language and at the end of that year he also talked French.'

But even if some children seem to be speaking a new language after only a couple of months, is this really so very quick? How, for instance, would this compare with an adult in the same situation? In fact it is not unlikely that an adult who is given the same amount of practice, who has a strong wish to communicate with everyone, and who has to master only a relatively restricted vocabulary – as is the case with children – will do equally well and possibly even better than a young child.

The notion that young children are so capable of quickly learning a new language seems to be derived from the fact that, at a young age, they are capable of learning so many skills in such a relatively short period of time. Like walking or eating with a spoon, learning a

47

language, or a second language, is one of those skills. But all parents grow accustomed to the fact that each child determines the speed with which she or he acquires each skill: some children are early walkers and late talkers, while others are early talkers and may develop physically at a slower speed. And, as with physical and mental development, one should allow for individual differences rather than make broad generalizations with regard to children's bilingual development.

Self-consciousness

It is also often thought that young children have a natural way of learning a second language, for they learn it the way children learn everything: by imitating, by participating, and last but not least, by not being self-conscious. Well, I want to argue that self-consciousness can start at a very early age. We all know that babies and toddlers often behave quite differently in the presence of strangers: some put on their sunniest face, others become stubborn or start crying. In any case, they know that they are being watched and react accordingly.

Indeed, self-consciousness can be both a positive and a negative asset for children in a bilingual situation. Clearly some children like being watched and they love applause. They are the ones that thrive, for they can please all those around them, whether they are parents, grandparents, or schoolteachers. But for those children who are rather more shy and withdrawn, the requirement to speak two different languages may minimize their sociability.

Not only do children behave in a self-conscious manner at certain times, but they are generally more conscious of the bilingual situation than is often suggested, and I am not the only mother who thinks this. Simone, whose experiences with her three-year-old daughter were discussed in the previous chapter, wrote:

'My daughter Nathalie is conscious that she can speak one language (i.e. French) and that another one (i.e. English) has to be learned. They do not both come entirely "naturally" despite the fact that she is "immersed".'

And what about learning through imitation and participation? A great amount of learning takes place through copying, but some children are known to choose an observer's role for quite a long time before they start participating and actually reproduce what they have learned. Schoolteachers have all seen pupils who have kept silent until they felt completely ready to express themselves adequately. As an experienced headmistress once told me: 'The longer they keep quiet, the more intelligent they are.' Maybe she only said this to reassure me, which it did, but the observation itself shows that not all children like to plunge into a new situation as active participants.

A native accent

It is considered to be one of the greatest rewards of a bilingual upbringing that children learn to speak each language with a native accent. For many people this provides one of the most compelling reasons for starting the bilingual experience at an early age. Otherwise, it is thought, it may be too late.

❡ As the English language gradually became a part of life for my own children, two things happened with their accents for which I hadn't been prepared at all. When Gideon started to speak English he did so with a distinctly Dutch accent, apparently because he was copying us in our contacts with the outside world rather than picking up the language straight from native speakers.

When my daughter Hedda first tried to communicate in English, she did this by speaking Dutch with an English accent, just hoping that other people would make some sense out of this! Now, when she speaks English, she does so with a more or less native accent, but in the meantime her accent in Dutch has definitely acquired an English flavour. ❡

So how true is it that children learn to speak with a native accent right from the beginning? And, if a child doesn't conform to this rule, is his or her way of responding very much of an exception?

Let us have a closer look at the assumption that children are capable of speaking a new language without an accent. The point about this assumption is that it only looks at the result and not at the process. The result is usually that children end up speaking the language of the country in which they live with a native accent, although they might also develop a 'foreign' accent in the language that is the mother tongue of one or both parents, even if this was the only language they spoke at all before starting to go to school. A number of parents reported this, recording a switch half-way: first the children spoke their home language as native speakers, but its accent could be traced in the language being learned at school; but, as soon as the latter one took over as the dominant language, the accent of the home language could become affected.

It seems, however, that the problem usually resolves itself as the children get older. Children who are being brought up bilingually from an early age can achieve a native accent in both languages, always provided that they get enough practice in both. But this result is not

49

reached automatically and parents should not be too surprised or too disappointed if, at least for a while, their child speaks with a funny accent in a language he or she is trying to master.

Some parents pointed out to me that children may have another little surprise in store concerning the accent they acquire in a language: they need not necessarily learn to speak with an accent that is considered to be the 'right' one. The local accent may differ considerably from the 'received pronunciation' that the parents were taught when studying the language at school or university. For some parents this may even be a cause for worry, but at least the accent acquired by the children will always be more of the real thing than most adult learners can ever hope to achieve.

A native accent can even be developed far away from its place of origin, as is illustrated by the following case. Carole is English, her husband is Italian, and they live in Switzerland. Both their children were born there and they are now fifteen and ten years old. Carole wrote:

'I am from Yorkshire and my boys have Yorkshire accents when they speak English, which of course amuses everybody.'

Playmates

❢ I can't remember how many times it was said to me when the children were little: "Oh, as soon as your children start playing with other children, they will learn to speak English." But I regularly noticed that other children weren't particularly interested in a new playmate who neither understood nor spoke their language. It is simply not true that all children automatically enjoy the company of all other children. Moreover, at times I myself found it pretty difficult to understand the halting and lisping talk of many of the three and four year olds around me, and I often wondered how my own children were supposed to learn English from them.

The fact that my children didn't pick up much English from their playmates was actually mirrored by those playmates themselves: I never heard one of them copy one single Dutch word from my children, even during play sessions where two out of three children were speaking almost exclusively Dutch. ❢

It is often argued that children pick up a language by playing with other children and it seems such a logical and easy way too. But at what age do children start using language as an important means of communication amongst themselves? At two? Not really. At three? Sometimes yes, sometimes not. At four, yes, language definitely plays a role.

❝ At age four, however, Gideon still happily played on his own and he actually preferred to withdraw from contact and to keep silent than to get frustrated by not being able to say something properly. Hedda, on her part, has always had many communicative skills and at three was beginning to use language as a means of making contact with other children. If her approach of speaking Dutch with an English accent didn't work, she would just resort to other means of communication, such as taking someone by the hand and pointing to whatever she wanted to have or wanted to do. ❞

When assessing the role of playmates in the bilingual development of children, one has to make a distinction between learning a language and practising its use. No doubt, playing with other children of the same age provides ample opportunity for a child to try out his or her knowledge of a language in a fairly uninhibited way. But first a child will have had to learn a language before it can practise it, and this is where parents, and later on teachers, are more important than children of the same age group. A similar observation was made in Chapter 3 in the section on visits and visitors: children can only really benefit from staying abroad if they already have a basic command of the 'other' language.

Language learning between children sometimes gets going when one child is somewhat older than the other. But, as social contacts for children usually start through playgroup or nursery school, it is not always easy to find suitable playmates from another age group. These circumstances particularly apply to an eldest child in a family. For second and third children the opportunity to learn from older ones is provided by their brothers and sisters and by the friends of those siblings, although the outcome of this situation can be quite different for individual families. So after discussing the role of playmates, let's now turn to siblings and their reactions to a bilingual environment.

Siblings

In single-language marriages, where the children have to learn the 'other' language through contact with the outside world, a second child sometimes has an easier time than the first one. Veronica, who earlier in the chapter described her first-born's experience of learning to cope with the French language at the age of two, noticed:

'Our second boy didn't have such problems, I think because he grew up in a bilingual environment more or less from the beginning and the way had been paved by his older brother.'

But the existence of an older brother or sister may also mean that the second one hardly gets a chance to become bilingual at all! Especially in mixed-language marriages, the language spoken by all the other children locally and at school may take over all too quickly. By the time the younger one begins to talk, the older child will have started to attend a playgroup or nursery school, and will bring home the language that is spoken there. And more often than not the children soon start communicating with each other in that language.

Annick and her family were introduced earlier in this book, in Chapter 2. She is always quite ready to share her thoughts with other people and she has a lot to say on the subject of bilingual children. On the whole, her experience seems to have been a positive one and she herself emphasizes that she has never had any regrets about sticking to her original idea of bringing up her children with two languages. But this was one of her experiences:

'It became much more difficult with Francesca, who is the youngest of our three children, because there was a bigger gap in age, and for a long time I thought she had missed the boat about speaking French. The other thing was that the other two would speak for her whenever she wanted something, and so she had it easy. She didn't have to make the effort, for the others would do it for her. And then there was so much English around at that time – also she felt very conscious that they could speak French and she couldn't. So all the time when she was little she didn't want to speak any French. But then, when she was about six or seven, she finally started speaking French and in some ways her accent was even better than the others, but maybe that's because of her better ear.'

For many a second or third child a bilingual upbringing can therefore appear to be less effective, and parents are faced with problems that didn't crop up when there was only one child. But I also believe that the child's own temperament and talents are at least as important in a bilingual development as the influence of older brothers or sisters.

This is illustrated by the following case in which two little boys were confronted with the same bilingual situation at the same time. The parents are both Dutch and the mother gave me a detailed account of the reactions of her two boys:

'Mark and Jelmer moved to England when they were four-and-a-half and two-and-a-half years old. From the very beginning they both attended playgroup, but they reacted quite differently. I remember that on our first visit to playgroup Mark, the older one, stepped forward to ask a question. He realized that a different language was being spoken, but he simply didn't care. Of course, Mark's first attempt at communication was greatly admired and encouraged by everyone and he quickly learned to speak English. I think his talent for communication was also illustrated by the fact that one month after he had started infant school all his classmates were copying and using his "pidgin" English.

'It was clear to me that Mark was never held back by shyness or self-consciousness in his social contacts, whatever language was being spoken. This was not true for his younger brother Jelmer, who didn't feel comfortable at all in his new environment. I decided to stop playgroup for him until he was three-and-a-half and had acquired some familiarity with English through watching television and socializing at home. After that I still spent considerable time settling him in his playgroup, until he felt confident enough to communicate in English by himself.'

Frustration

Children have a strong need to communicate, and as they get older language becomes an increasingly important means of communication. If they sense that they can't express themselves adequately, they are bound to feel less than happy about it. Their frustration can express itself in many different ways, and one possible reaction is aggressive behaviour. A number of mothers told me that they had noticed how their own children reacted aggressively towards other children because of their unsuccessful attempts to communicate.

Again, this shows that the presence of other children is not an automatic guarantee for learning a new language. It can also be the reason why meeting 'foreign' children during holidays is not always as productive as parents would like. A German father who lives in England told me the following story about his small son:

'He does speak a bit of German, but once when we had a German family staying with us for a short holiday, he was upset and angry that the other children didn't speak English. He knew and had accepted the fact that grown-ups sometimes have this funny habit of talking in a foreign language, but surely all children spoke English!'

As they become more aware of the bilingual situation, many children experience some difficulty in their efforts to communicate, for instance during their first time at nursery school or when visiting their cousins abroad. I found that it helped my children when I explained to them that they in fact had an extra ability that many other children didn't have, namely to express themselves in two languages. If children do realize this, and I think children of three and four can understand this quite well, it may compensate for the feelings of inadequacy they sometimes have to cope with.

It's all a game

At the beginning of this chapter I mentioned that a number of parents who are bringing up their children with two languages did indeed answer 'yes', or even 'certainly', to my question whether they agreed with the opinion that learning a second language comes quickly and easily for young children. I would therefore like to conclude this chapter by quoting one of them.

A parent who wrote quite enthusiastically about the bilingual upbringing of his children was David. He is English and his wife comes from the French-speaking part of Belgium. They live in Holland. He wrote about his three-year-old and one-year-old daughters:

'The first child is bilingual. Why? Because she gets along fine in both English and Dutch (understanding and speaking: she doesn't yet read and write herself). The second is not yet truly lingual.'

And he concluded:

'It's early days yet: a lot can change in the child's own attitudes (perhaps). At the moment it's absolutely no problem, though. It's a fact of life and it's fun. Our daughter can also sing a few French songs. It's all a game – so far.'

7
In the middle – bilingualism for 5–11 year olds

The bilingual development of children between the ages of five and eleven has its own special problems. The home environment is no longer the single most important influence and there is no guarantee yet that both languages will survive. One mother tried to convince me that age five was the absolute peak-time for crisis. Another mother, who had moved from one country to another when her children were nine and ten years old, was quite taken aback by the speed at which her children seemed to be forgetting their original mother tongue.

The language spoken at school will become the dominant language and the important question during this period is whether the other language will survive school and peer-group influence. When the children are small, keeping up both languages is sometimes hard work for the parents. Now, during this period, the children themselves have to make an effort as well, but they may also begin to experience some of the benefits.

Feeling different

Primary school age is the time when children build up an image of themselves, and it becomes increasingly important to them how other people perceive them. Peer-group influence begins to grow stronger and many children don't want to feel different from other children in their class. Many parents reported signs of their children becoming embarrassed when they had to speak the 'other' language in front of other people, and parents would consequently be instructed by their children never to speak 'that language', except at home.

Zoë moved from Greece to England as a student. She met her Greek husband in London, where they have stayed ever since. They have always made a conscious effort to keep up the Greek language with their children. She remembered:

'My daughter didn't want me to speak Greek to her at all when I picked her up from school. It was embarrassing for her to use that language in front of her friends.'

But as we have seen in the previous chapter, siblings need not react in the same way, for Zoë also told me:

55

'Dimitri, however, who is quite a bit younger than her, reacted in a totally opposite way. He would shout out in Greek to me when coming out of school, just to boast to his friends about his ability to speak a foreign language.'

Feeling different may be experienced as something positive or as something negative, but it is almost always an important issue for this age group. It may help when parents talk to their children about the family's bilingual situation and explain about the different languages that are being spoken by relatives who live in other countries. One father who did exactly that was Bruno. He comes from Switzerland and his mother tongue is German. He and his French wife live in France and they have two children who are now seven and five years old. They were both brought up with French as their first language. He wrote:

'When my son was little and started speaking French, he could not understand why his grandparents in Switzerland did not speak the same language as he did. We explained to him that he had to learn German. Now, when he manages to express himself in German, he realizes that German-speaking people understand him. He seems to be proud.'

And also:

'Generally, I do not think they feel different from other children; but occasionally they want to let their friends know that they know something more than them.'

Being able to speak a second language can also create a special bond between parents and children, and between siblings. The self-image they are developing and the confidence some children build up during this age sometimes induces them to start using the foreign language as a 'secret' language. Instead of being embarrassed, they become a bit cheeky and use the foreign language with their parents or siblings whenever they want to keep something private. I don't think it is at all harmful for a child to find out that knowing another language can give some sort of power, instead of experiencing it as something that stands in the way of being like all the other children.

Learning to read

If we talk about bilingualism for children, do we mean that they just have to be able to speak two languages or should they also be capable of reading both of them? One of the major issues in the language development of children from five years upwards is learning to read. How difficult is it to read a second language once you have mastered the technique of reading one?

First of all, not all parents who like their children to be bilingual also want them to be able to read in two languages, at least not at a young age. Many parents are happy to wait until the foreign language is taught at school, at which time the reading skill is developed automatically. However, the age at which foreign-language teaching starts at school varies in different countries. Usually foreign languages are not taught until secondary school level, but sometimes English or French is added to the curriculum at an earlier stage. In either case the situation is relatively simple as far as developing a reading skill in two languages is concerned.

However, there is a whole range of languages which are not taught at regular local schools at all. Sometimes there is the opportunity for children to attend a special school on Saturdays, where they learn to read and write in the mother tongue of one or both parents. But these schools are only available in some places and for some languages, so it is not a solution that many parents can rely on.

When and how, then, should a child learn to read in two languages when the parents themselves are the only possible teachers? I found that it was more often the parents in single-language marriages who wanted their children to start reading the language that is spoken at home as soon as possible. But most of these parents also agreed that reading in the two respective languages should be learned consecutively, first one language and then the other, rather than two languages at the same time.

Which language the child will first learn to read depends on the individual child and on the age at which formal reading lessons are started at school. If a child is interested in books and seems eager to find out about the technique of reading, you might decide as a parent to teach him or her the alphabet and the sounds of the language spoken at home before he or she learns to read at school. But teaching your child how to read is not something all parents like to undertake and many prefer to wait until a child has learned the basic skill at school. When a child has had a fair amount of reading practice in one language, then is probably the best time for a parent to sit down with his or her child and explain the intricacies of reading the other language.

Reading in two languages requires books in two languages. And parents may encounter some problems here. For instance, the Hungarian and Polish mothers I talked to complained about a general lack of appropriate reading material for their children. Even if they were sufficiently in touch with their respective home countries, they didn't particularly like the kind of books that were available.

Another relevant observation – put forward by one of the parents – is that, sooner or later, the language development in the foreign language, the language not spoken at school, will come to a point where it is no longer on a par with the age development of the child. The vocabulary used in the books that are intended for their age group is then too difficult. The result is that they are either forced to read books below their interest level or constantly have to be helped along with more interesting but more difficult material.

It is not always easy to find a practical solution to these problems. Moreover, it all depends on the child's capabilities and her or his interests. But, as with speaking another language, practice is needed to develop and maintain a good reading skill. One mother told me that the only thing her son would read in the foreign language was weather forecasts, as these happened to interest him a great deal. And, as we saw in Chapter 5, another mother managed to provide ample reading material for her three sons by buying them Spanish comics, while not allowing English comics in the house.

Survival

As was just mentioned, a particular feature of the bilingual development of children in this age group is the growing discrepancy between age development and language development. The language spoken at school will almost always become the language in which the children learn more complex notions, in which they are capable of reading more interesting books, and in which they can express themselves more accurately. As a result they will also want to use this language at home to describe and ask questions about their expanding world.

Yannis is Greek, but his wife is English. The family live in London, and Yannis told me this about his experience with his six-year-old son:

'He seems to be moving into the adult world very fast these days. He asks all these questions about "how the bank works" and "what is democracy", and he asks them in English. I believe that as a parent one has an important role, to answer these questions. I used to talk to him in Greek quite regularly, but now it is becoming clear that his command of that language is not good enough for discussing these subjects. So I find myself talking to him in English more and more often.'

In this situation there is clearly a risk that English will completely take over and that the use, and even knowledge, of Greek will disappear altogether. But I think that it is more important for parents and children to be able to communicate with each other, in whatever language or languages, than to set rigid rules about keeping up a language at all times. It seems to me that parents and children who have managed to overcome most of the initial difficulties of keeping up two languages will also get by during these years.

The time has now come, though, for parents to set themselves a 'long-term' goal with respect to the bilingual upbringing. Even if the two languages don't play an equal role in daily life, there should always remain an awareness for all the members of the family that the foreign language is particularly relevant at some times and at some places. Visits and visitors, as described in Chapter 3, are now of vital importance in retaining a natural link with the language.

Judging by the families I have come to know, it is my impression that children who have acquired a basic skill in a second language by the time they go to primary school will become and remain reasonably bilingual – always provided they have a fair chance of practising this language during holidays abroad and with relatives who come to visit. Even if the use of the second language seems to disappear almost completely from daily life, the ability to use it will remain and can again be built upon whenever and wherever needed.

Hard work and benefits

Although it is possible to become and remain fluent in two languages, it doesn't always come easy. The following observation came from a French mother who migrated to England with her children some six years ago to marry an Englishman. The children are now between seven and eleven years old. She said:

'My children are French children who happen to live in England. For them it means they want to succeed at both ends. They go to school in England, where they have to speak English and behave English. They spend most of their holidays in France, where their relatives live and where some of their closest friends are. There they speak French and also want to be in line with their peer group. As yet I don't think they appreciate the advantages. For them it sometimes just means hard work.'

It is difficult to establish at what age children themselves begin to experience the advantages of having two languages. It is not enough that parents keep telling their children how useful the other language is or stress that they have a capability that many other children haven't. It is probably not until the bilingual situation actually brings a few rewards for them that the children themselves will start enjoying it. Annick had the following comments on the situation for her children during their primary school years:

'Occasionally, when Marc was younger, he didn't like me to speak French, because vis-à-vis his friends he didn't want to feel different. But if he was with foreign children, then he didn't mind at all, because he knew it was normal for them also to be different. It was only if he was just with his peer group at school.

'But most people were always admiring the children for being bilingual and so on and in some ways they quite liked that. They felt a bit special and that compensated for it. I should also add that they have many French cousins and they inherited all the nice things from them. They always got nice clothes and all the toys, so it had a nice flavour, French, because it was linked with getting presents. And on our holidays in France, they were always made to feel very special, because they were the English ones, the only ones who didn't speak the same language. It made it much more positive from their point of view. Every time they went to France, they were treated as kings and queens.'

Moving abroad

When children are still little, it seems relatively easy to migrate with them, while the problems that migration would create for teenagers with respect to their education and social life are quite obvious. For children of primary school age, however, many parents are not sure just what the advantages and disadvantages might be. We already came across an example of moving abroad with children of this age in Chapter 3, where we talked about changing circumstances, and the following account is very instructive with respect to the consequences of a temporary move for the child concerned.

The permanent home of Françoise and her English husband is in London, but they lived abroad for a few years.

'Catherine was six when we moved to the French-speaking part of Belgium, while her older brother stayed in England and her younger sister was still very young. She obviously suffered most, being transplanted twice right in the middle of primary school. But, of the three children, she definitely ended up with the best command of both languages.

'At the time she knew a bit of French, for I had spoken it to the children when they were little. I remember that she worked quite hard and that after six months she had caught up and even became first in her class. But it was much more difficult when we came back to England after almost four years. Although she could still speak and understand English, she could not read or write it very well. It took her quite a bit longer to catch up than when she was little. We also found that at age ten it is not just a matter of language. At school they are supposed to have a whole range of general knowledge which they haven't got when they first arrive in a new country.'

In many respects it may seem easier to move abroad or to travel around when the children are still quite young. But – as I myself experienced with my own children and as we saw in the previous chapter – some small children also find it difficult to adapt to changing circumstances.

In the following case primary school age became, in fact, the consolidating period for the child involved. Gert and Trine are both Danish, but they lived in quite a few different places all over the world before they settled in London. They took turns in telling me how it all happened:

'In principle Danish is the language of the house, but we have never been too strict about it, as it was difficult enough for Jacob to keep up with the changing circumstances. And it hasn't been easy for him.'

'He was born in England, but soon afterwards we moved back to Denmark. When he was eighteen months old and just starting to talk, we moved to Saudi Arabia for a year, where he went to an English-speaking nursery school. He didn't talk while he was there and just played his time away.'

'At age two-and-a-half we were in Denmark for six weeks and there he picked up Danish very fast. Then we went to England, where again he attended an English nursery school. It was awful, he just was totally lost for a while. And by the time he got confident in English we moved again, this time to Nigeria for six months.'

'Now we have finally settled in London and he goes to a very good local primary school. He is OK now. He speaks English as any child of his age would do; he understands Danish, and sometimes he will speak it too.'

An authority

The influence of school and the school environment is often substantial. But with regard to language use parents should be prepared to face yet another consequence of the bilingual situation in which they have put themselves and their children. As soon as children start going to school, their command of the local language might begin to exceed that of a 'foreign' parent. The latter should not then be too surprised if a child starts making comments about the parent's use of the language spoken outside the house. And if this parent has been in the habit of regularly correcting the child's language use, the roles can now become reversed!

❝ I myself will never forget the moment that Gideon for the first time corrected my pronunciation of an English word. It happened a few months after he had started primary school, around his fifth birthday.

At the time his English vocabulary was still limited, but the words he did know, he was obviously quite sure about. Actually, I didn't believe he was right and looked it up in the dictionary. It turned out that he was right and I knew that from then on he was developing into an authority on English usage in our house. **❜**

8

In search of identity – bilingual teenagers

During the interviews, my order of questions was as follows: first, I always asked how the parents thought and felt about the subject. Then I would ask them how their children reacted when they were small, when they started going to school, and when they grew older and became critical teenagers. However, I decided that it was not enough to ask only the parents about their children's reactions, but that I should let a number of the older ones speak for themselves. As children approach their teens, they begin to question most of the things they have been brought up with, and one can expect that they also start questioning the bilingual situation.

At first I felt a bit nervous when faced with the task of interviewing teenagers. What exactly should I ask them and how would they react to my questions? In my daily life I hardly ever deal directly with youngsters of that age and I wasn't quite sure how to approach them. However, not only did I enjoy talking to these teenagers far more than I expected, it also became evident that the case they put forward is on the whole a positive one and that there is no doubt that a bilingual upbringing can bring some of the benefits that parents hope to attain for their children.

Being bilingual, or not

The parents of all these teenagers had been interviewed by me on an earlier occasion, so I already knew a bit about their backgrounds and about their bilingual development in earlier years. As with their parents, the first question I always asked was: 'Do you consider yourself to be bilingual?'

Again, we have to remember that it is very difficult to pin down exactly what bilingualism is and when it is achieved, because it is a process rather than a state. As one mother wrote:

'Each child is different: some learn effortlessly at first and experience difficulties later – and the reverse is also true. Some never master the second language ... some master speaking, but never reading or writing, and so on. The permutations are endless!'

But also again, if it is difficult to define bilingualism, this doesn't

63

prevent individuals from having their own ideas about it. When I went to interview fifteen-year-old Dimitri, his twenty-year-old sister Joanna was also in London, at home from university, and I used the opportunity to talk to her as well. She declared:

'Yes, I am bilingual, because I speak Greek fluently and feel at ease when I am in Greece talking to Greek people.'

For teenagers who are born and raised in one and the same country there is no need to reflect on their mastery of the language spoken at school. Obviously that is the language they know best and which they take for granted. The fluency in the other language, the one spoken at home and/or with their relatives abroad, is the measuring stick for their degree of bilingualism. This is true even if it used to be the other way around when they were small, and the foreign language was the one they learned first – which is the case with Joanna and Dimitri, for they were born in England but both their parents are Greek. They were brought up with Greek as their first language and had to learn English when they started going to school, but English has long taken over as the dominant language. When asked about his feelings on being bilingual, Dimitri had the following observation:

'I've had this experience of speaking Greek in Greece and people looking at me as if I was quite stupid. I think this is because I speak with a proper Greek accent and sound like a Greek kid, but at the same time I don't know lots of ordinary phrases. They say this will happen less often as you get older, for then people realize more quickly that you don't speak the language quite the way they do and they appreciate more your efforts of trying.'

But let's not forget, while there are many teenagers – with one or two parents from abroad – who end up being bilingual, there are also many who don't. I talked to a few of them to find out how they felt. Sixteen-year-old Kevin has a German mother and was brought up in England. His reaction:

'No, I am not bilingual. Why? Because I can't speak two languages. But yeah, I suppose I have some mixed feelings about it. On the one hand I would like to learn German, on the other hand I just can't take the first step. If I could snap my fingers and there it was, I wouldn't mind being bilingual. Maybe my mum should have pushed a bit harder when I was young, but for me it's too late now.'

Growing awareness

We can never predict how and when our children will react to the bilingual home environment, and a growing awareness of a multilingual and multicultural background can take many forms. Some teenagers may start brooding over their own and their parents' origins, others tend to treat everything rather as a matter of fact, while again others may be quite proud of being somewhat different from the rest.

Being a mother of two teenagers herself, Birgitte had this general comment:

'I think it can give them a certain kudos among their friends: cosmopolitan and smarter than the homebirds. If they are confident and settled in their own culture, this can be a distinct advantage and help foster their interest. If they are not, it may provide a most unwholesome escape route from social and personal responsibility.'

Birgitte is Danish and lives in London with an English husband. She gave up speaking Danish to her own children a long time ago. But, since the children have become older, she sees an opportunity of renewing the interest on their part. This is what she wrote about her eighteen-year-old son:

'I just took him to Denmark for a week and now he is seriously interested in the country, the language and the culture – and he was happier than I have seen him for a long time: he was approaching a part of himself and his own background as a thinking adult. I think it worked!'

Some of the teenagers I talked to were very thoughtful and articulate. At an age when parents often wonder if their offspring think at all, let alone think seriously, I found that these children were all taking stock of their particular background. Sixteen-year-old Alex was born in England, but his mother Angelika as well as his father come from Germany. He told me:

'I feel I am a German person born and raised in England. Over the years I have had strong anti-British feelings and I have idolized Germany. But it was always the nice times, the holidays, that were spent in Germany, and I know that I would have been more critical of a lot of things had I actually lived there. As a matter of fact, I am rather critical of many Western ideas and ideals. To me, Germany is a bit like a dream. I like to have the "other possibility", the fact that I have friends there and that I could live there for a shorter or longer period of time if I wanted to. Still, I am not bilingual. Understanding German is OK, but I don't speak it very easily. Sometimes I find myself being embarrassed, because I can't speak German as well as I should.'

Learning languages at school

As they approach their teens, children may increasingly appreciate the advantages of being bilingual, if only because it means getting high marks when taking the second language as a subject at school. But the way a language is taught at school is very different from the way it is being picked up in a bilingual home environment. This is often felt as a drawback when first starting to learn the language at school, which is why one mother actually advised against taking such lessons.

Ursula comes from Germany, while her husband is English. They lived in several countries all over the world before they finally settled down in London sixteen years ago. They are both teachers: she teaches German, and he has always taught English as a foreign language. Three of their children are already in their twenties, while two are still teenagers. For all of them German was the language they learned first. Ursula seemed to speak from long experience when she said:

'Children can't learn their mother tongue as if it were a foreign language. The vocabulary taught at school is different, the accent spoken by the teacher is probably quite different and, if teacher and pupil are not particularly aware of the discrepancy and the reasons for it, it will end up in a struggle and the child will get confused. In my view, children should just get familiar with the type of exam they have to take. If necessary, and if possible, a parent should supply some formal instruction for the occasion and then the child should be left to tackle the material in his or her own way.'

Obviously, this advice is worthwhile only if the child concerned is already quite fluent in the second language, reading and writing as well as speaking, and it also very much depends on the type of knowledge and the level expected for the exam.

Nevertheless Ursula's remarks illustrate the differences between the home and school environment when learning a language is involved. And perhaps they also explain why the teenagers I talked to didn't find learning a third or fourth language particularly easy. Eighteen-year-old Anja thought she speaks German well enough to call herself bilingual English–German, but she had the following comment on learning languages at school:

'At home I never learned German in relation to grammar, which made it difficult at first, and I think the teacher found me irritating, for I kept using different words to those taught at school. Learning French didn't go well at all, for I found I had to start from the beginning and the way I had to learn the language was so different. Also, I never stayed in France long enough to pick up the language in a natural way, as I did with German.'

From my conversations with teenagers, it appeared once again that bilingual children with a talent for languages will enjoy learning a third or fourth language. However, those who are not particularly language-minded may regard being bilingual a special bonus, but they would still have to make quite an effort to learn any other foreign languages. Also, if one isn't particularly good at languages, one might have more difficulties in keeping the two languages apart. As one of them remarked:

'My English and French have affected each other and, especially in writing, there is always this transfer. I feel that the fact that I know French relatively well hasn't made me brilliant in English.'

Problems

I had always thought that teasing other children was something that took place particularly during primary school years. But when I asked my informants whether coming from a bilingual background had ever made them feel different from other children and whether they remembered any specific reactions from people around them, several of them brought up the fact that they had sometimes been teased by their classmates in the early years of secondary school. Alex:

'I did get the occasional mockery, but after a while you get used to it. In a way it made me feel superior and I never retaliated. I think it even built up my German ego. These days it is still picked out sometimes, as each person has something that can be commented on, but always in a friendly way. We all make jokes about each other, but they aren't meant to offend.'

Each person experiences the bilingual situation in a different way and problems with the two languages or with one's search for identity may arise at various stages in one's development. Moreover, as I already stressed in the previous chapters, the same situation can be experienced as problematic by one child and as unproblematic by another. One mother told me that her son had had a difficult time all the way through primary school, but now, at sixteen, was very proud and completely at ease with his international background. At the same time, her younger daughter, who had always been easygoing, had started to blame her mixed background for all her troubles now that she was in her teens.

Parents will watch these developments and will try to help their children to sort things out. But their children's reactions may also make parents doubt whether they took the right decision in the first place, and often they don't know until the children have grown quite a bit older. Let's hear what Joanna had to say about this. She could still remember that she hardly spoke any English when she first started school:

'It actually was quite a nightmare. I spoke practically no English and I just couldn't communicate. My way of attracting attention was making a fuss, being naughty and all that. I got very little understanding or patience from my teachers or the other school kids. I think it took me two or three years, until I was about seven, before I felt absolutely confident at school and I knew I was equally fluent in English as all the other kids.'

She then added:

'My parents kept telling me how lucky I was, but it took me quite a while before I thought so myself. Now I'm grateful that they stuck to it, but certainly that hasn't always been the case.'

Two languages – two cultures

I think that many parents hope that bringing up their children with two languages will also mean that they will become familiar with two cultures. So I asked the teenagers whether they thought that knowing a different language is just a matter of knowing different words and phrases or that the other language tells you something about the other culture as well.

Sixteen-year-old Christopher has an English father and a French mother. He was born and brought up in England, but over the years he has spent practically all his holidays in France. He told me:

'If you inherit a language, you associate yourself with the country it comes from, the culture and the way people live there. At school they only teach "wars" when talking about other countries. I don't really know other European countries, but I know I feel English when in England and I feel French when in France.'

Quite a number of parents mentioned the fact that they considered themselves to be an international or European family rather than belonging to one particular country or nationality. One of them was Annick, for she said:

'The fact that we live in London is in a way accidental. I am French and my husband was brought up in England, but he comes from a German background. We probably would prefer to live on the continent, but jobwise that is impossible. I'm very happy that our children speak both French and English, and now we have even started to teach them a bit of German.'

Parents and children may be part of one and the same family, but they need not always have the same feelings about knowing different languages or having a multicultural background. When I asked fifteen-year-old Marc, the eldest of Annick's children, where he would prefer to live in later life, he replied:

'England or North America. It's got nothing to do with the language and nothing really with the people, but I get a bit bored when we are in France. I like it really a lot in England and when we went to live in

Canada for a year, it was great fun too. So I wouldn't mind living over there either.'

I couldn't help smiling when I heard this. Annick herself had warned me that Marc would probably play down the possible benefits of his bilingual background, and here it was.

Other teenagers gave answers that were more in line with their parents' views. And when they formulated them as well as Dominic, they argued convincingly in favour of bilingualism. Dominic is fifteen. He was born in England, he has a Spanish mother and an English father. He is the middle one of three boys. His mother Angelina, who was present during the interview, commented that 'he was always so casual about things'. At the same time it was clear that she was quite proud of the way he handled the bilingual and bicultural situation. Dominic told me:

'I think the biggest advantage of it all is that I am familiar with two cultures. It has taught me to see any subject from two points of view. You can always understand why someone sees something different than you do. Also, because I speak Spanish, I really have a chance to find out things for myself when I am in Spain, especially now that I am a bit older. The fact that my mother doesn't have to act as an interpreter means that I don't have to see and experience things through her.'

Passing it on

As I mentioned in Chapter 4, parents who themselves were brought up with two languages don't always want to do the same thing with their children. So I wondered how these teenagers would feel about continuing the tradition and whether this would tell us something about their appreciation of the bilingual experience. Would it be 'never again' or would they want to pass it on?

The idea of passing on the bilingual tradition to one's children did appeal to almost all the the teenagers I spoke to. 'Yes, but I'll leave that to granny', said one, and 'All of it', said another. One of them, however, gave a rather precise and cautious answer to this question. Joanna:

'Maybe I would like to teach them Greek if and when I have children of my own. But I think it is pretty difficult to do in any other situation than the one my parents were in, and this is that you both come from the same foreign country. My case would certainly not be the same, because my relationship with the language is different. If I marry an English person, I would be the only one to speak Greek, and it wouldn't even be my best language. Therefore I think it would never be an easy or natural thing to do.'

I have often wondered whether bilingualism – or rather the inclination to move abroad or to marry someone who comes from another country – is something that runs in families. Quite a few of the parents I talked to not only came from a bilingual background themselves, but also had brothers or sisters who had moved abroad too or who had embarked on a mixed-language marriage. Moreover, I met a number of parents who did not come from a bilingual background, but who mentioned the fact that they also had a brother or sister who – through migration or marriage – had created a bilingual home environment for their children.

If we take this into account, it is not unlikely that quite a few of these teenagers will in fact do the same thing: go and live abroad and/or marry someone from another country and thus pass on the tradition of a bilingual home environment to their children.

9
The role of mothers

In a bilingual upbringing the parties concerned are parents and children, and in the preceding chapters we have examined the role and reactions of both. Up to this point I have referred to individual parents by using their first names, or by saying 'one mother commented'. In this way I have always distinguished between mothers and fathers, but without giving an explicit reason for doing so. Now it's time to explain why I think it is important in a discussion of bringing up children in a bilingual home environment to differentiate between mothers and fathers.

One of the questions I asked all the parents was: do you as a mother/father have a different role in the bilingual upbringing of your children than your husband/wife as a father/mother? Interestingly, I have found that mothers and fathers do indeed have different roles with respect to the bilingual development of their children, even if they themselves don't always recognize this.

I think there are really two reasons for distinguishing between the roles of mothers and fathers. First, the parent who stays at home to look after the child or children – and, at the time of writing, this is generally the mother – is always more closely involved in the bilingual upbringing. Almost all the mothers I talked to said that, because they were more around, they felt more responsible than their husbands for dealing with the two languages in their house. They said they thought about it more and they worried more.

Secondly, if a mother does go out to work, she still feels that she is the one who is responsible for making a success of the bilingual upbringing, probably as part and parcel of the general anxiety as to whether the children are 'suffering' in any way. Mothers take this responsibility upon themselves but, as long as society expects women to look after the children, mothers are also subject to pressure from outside for the successful or not so successful bilingual development of their offspring.

Motherhood

In many of the families with mixed-language marriages that I visited, the wife was the partner from abroad. In those cases the bilingual upbringing seemed very much a mother's issue: if she decided to teach her children her own language, it was up to her to do so; if she had chosen not to give it a try, no one else would do the job for her. The degree of the father's involvement or support of course made a difference, but in general it was the mother who was faced with the problems and dilemmas involved.

Some of the women I interviewed had originally moved to a new country on their own in order to study or because of a job. By the time they met their partner, they were already somewhat familiar with many of the new circumstances and they probably had made some friends of their own. Other women had settled in a new country upon marriage and, if a baby arrived pretty soon after that, the first few years abroad were not always easy. A young and inexperienced mother who has to adapt to a new country, with few friends or relatives around, faces a monumental task which can take up all the energy and confidence she can muster. Being at home with young children and feeling rather isolated can therefore have the result that a failure of the bilingual upbringing is felt very acutely by a mother, as it seems to affect her as a person.

Lotte has lived in the small university town in the North of England since shortly after her marriage. She remembered:

'At the time, I was adamant that my children should know my language and my culture. Also, I felt I couldn't talk to children in English – if I knew how to talk to children at all. And, by the time Tom started playgroup, he had both Danish and English, for until then I had always spoken Danish to him and his father always English. Pretty soon after that, however, he decided to ignore Danish. He would simply pretend he hadn't heard me or didn't understand me. At the time I felt as if he was rejecting me and not just the language. I was pregnant with my second baby and still had a hard time trying to feel at home in this place where we live. It meant that I gave up the Danish.'

Pregnancy and childbirth are facts of life which are seldom taken into account in a discussion of bilingualism. Yet, they are part of a mother's experience. Being pregnant or having a young baby means a shift in one's priorities. And a struggle with a stubborn toddler who doesn't comply with his or her mother's bilingual plans may be the last thing a mother wants to deal with.

Birgitte told me she had had a similar experience with her children when they were little. In the previous chapter we came across Birgitte's remarks on teenagers in general, and on her own teenagers in particular. We also saw that she had given up speaking Danish to her children a long time ago, but she said she could still remember how it had all happened:

'I started off by speaking Danish to my first baby. Jonathan, however, kept silent until he spent a fortnight with an English family when he was just over two years old. I didn't give up speaking Danish straightaway, but gradually the language of the house became completely English, especially when Jonathan and his younger sister were old enough to talk English to each other. For me, speaking Danish to them acquired the character of my giving them language lessons rather than of us communicating with each other. And that wasn't the kind of relationship with my children that I was after.'

A first-time mother with a non-talking two-year-old on her hands might well begin to wonder whether she is doing the right thing by trying to instil two languages in an obstinate toddler. But slow starters aren't necessarily less competent or less interested at a later age: the same toddler who refused to speak Danish is now a young adult and he is considering going to live in Denmark for a while to learn the language properly and to keep his double nationality. Also, he himself commented that 'one of these days' he would sit down with a Danish grammar, as he felt that he would now benefit from a more academic approach.

Dual responsibility

Mothers are the watchdogs over the bilingual development of their children. There is so much more to a mother's role in the bilingual upbringing of her children than making the initial choice or just being around and speaking her own language. It takes skill, imagination, and perseverance on her part to achieve her goal. And what that goal is, is up to each mother to define for herself.

Judy and her husband are both English. I visited her in Amsterdam, where they live, and we had a long conversation about the bilingual upbringing of our children. Her experience resembles my own in many ways, not least because her daughter and my son are exactly the same age and have reacted quite similarly. Her story:

'When my daughter was born four years ago, I used to worry quite a bit about how she would cope with learning Dutch and it has not always been easy for her. It has taken her a long time to learn the language, although she has been with Dutch people almost from the very beginning. First she went to a childminder for a couple of hours each week, then she went to a playgroup from about eighteen months onwards and later to a proper nursery school.

'I have been fairly strict in keeping the two languages separate. I always just used English with her, but there have been occasions when I wanted to teach her some Dutch so that she could ask for certain things at school. For this purpose I would play a game with her and pretend that I was her schoolteacher who would then talk to her in Dutch. I have taken recourse to this 'technique' only a few times and now that she has a better grasp of both languages we don't seem to need it any longer. As she is getting older, she gets more competent and more confident. I feel that in a way she is less conscious of the fact that there are two different languages around, for they are no longer a barrier to what she wants to say or wants to do.'

I have found that many mothers living in a bilingual situation feel that they carry the responsibility for their children to succeed in both languages. If they speak to the children in their own language, they nevertheless want to make sure that those children understand and speak the local language by the time they go to school. The following example shows that this is not always an easy task, and it seems that avoiding a difficulty at one time may sometimes result in another problem later on.

Maïthé is French, while her husband is Dutch. I spoke to both of them when I visited them in Utrecht, a town in the centre of the Netherlands. They met in France, where they got married. Soon after they had moved to Holland, their first daughter was born and, as their common language had always been French, Maïthé didn't yet speak sufficient Dutch to use that language with her baby. She told me:

'When my older daughter started playgroup at two-and-a-half, she spoke very little Dutch and had difficulties in adapting. I felt quite sorry for her and began to speak Dutch to her at home more and more. In a way I felt she should learn proper Dutch from her father, but he liked practising his French at home. When our second daughter started talking, I taught her only Dutch, to avoid difficulties at school. The result was that, unlike her sister, she couldn't communicate with her French grandmother when she came to visit us.'

But it is not only language that a mother is concerned with. It is a matter of integrating her child in a way that suits both her own and her child's needs. This can, for instance, mean that she decides not to speak in her own language to the child, but that she still tries to teach her or him some of the children's songs that she grew up with. It can also mean that a mother makes a special effort to teach her children the local songs and rhymes, which she first has to learn herself. Let's hear what Angelina, the Spanish mother whose experiences have also been described earlier in this book, had to say about this. She clearly remembered the position in which she found herself:

'I wanted my children to learn Spanish and that was the language in which I talked to them from the beginning. At the same time I felt a great need to practise my English which was rather poor at the time. James was my first audience when I read aloud to him in English to get familiar with the language. Moreover, his father being English, I solemnly pledged that James would not miss out on any English nursery rhymes and songs, which were part of the world in which he was to grow up.'

An expanding world

When a child is little, the home environment is the most important influence, and so is the language spoken there. But the outside world begins right on the doorstep and gradually it will open up for the child. After a while all the influences of the outside world – including the language – will be brought into the home by the child to be tested there.

Angelika came from Germany to England almost twenty years ago, with her husband who was also German. I quoted her earlier in the book, where she talked about being or not being bilingual. She was the first person I interviewed and, by being very explicit in her views, she helped me a great deal to clarify my own thoughts on the whole subject of a bilingual upbringing. She told me:

'I think the location where we lived at the time was very important and had a lot to do with how we communicated with the children. We had a communal garden at the back of our flat which was very large, there were twenty houses on either side backing on to it, and there were several families with small children. So the peer group was extremely relevant, right from the word go. It was very difficult for me and later on impossible to keep up the German because of this. I would have very silly talks with the children like when I would say "this is called *Schere*, which is the German word for *scissors*, and they would insist that it was *scissors*. We would then end up in a "yes, no, yes it is, no it isn't" kind of argument.

'So we opted more and more for English, and the German spoken in the house became accidental. At that time I also began to read to them in English a lot because, once I realized I was fighting a losing battle against the peer group or the English environment, I felt I might just as well integrate them properly.'

In single-language marriages the wish to preserve the mother tongue will often be equally strong for both partners. Yet the dilemma for a parent who is at home with the children is different from that for a parent who is in a position to keep home and job separate.

For a parent who works away from home the two languages can belong to two really different spheres of life and switching from one language to the other needs to be done only twice a day. Someone who stays at home is in a totally different position. One may find oneself switching between the two languages many times during the day, and then it is not always easy to be consistent with the children. As one mother commented:

'Sometimes it just seems too easy for a father to be strict in wanting to keep up the mother tongue. If I invite children and other mothers over to our house, the language will soon be all English. If we don't socialize, I and the children remain isolated.'

Staying at home

If it is difficult at present for mothers to find a job and to go out to work, then it seems even more difficult for 'foreign mothers' to do so. By far the majority of mothers I talked to stayed at home when the children were young. One reason may be that foreign qualifications are not considered valid by prospective employers, but another reason is that childminding is a much more complicated issue when living in a new country.

❢ In my own experience, without having relatives or long-standing friends nearby, it can even be an effort to find an occasional babysitter. There may be a large supply of local teenagers, but they don't speak the language of my children. My two little ones would have been quite frightened and upset if someone unable to communicate with them had come over to babysit. ❢

With regard to a bilingual upbringing, staying at home with the children when they are young has advantages and disadvantages. The obvious advantage is that it gives a mother ample opportunity to teach her children her own language. Her continuous presence will guarantee that her mother tongue becomes the first language of the child, even if sooner or later the language of the outside world will take over as the dominant one.

We met Simone before in Chapter 5, when the one-person-one-language method was discussed. She wrote:

'I wanted my daughter to be able to speak both languages so that it would not make any difference to her if we stayed in England or decided to go to live in France – also, for immediate communication when on holidays with friends or family. I thought it was important enough for me to give up my job while the learning process was taking place.'

And later, as an answer to my question whether she thought she had a different role from her husband in the bilingual upbringing of their child, she wrote:

'No, except for the fact that I have chosen not to work in order to give my child a chance to become bilingual.'

A disadvantage of staying at home with the children could well be that a mother's exclusive use of her original tongue isolates her more than she would like. One mother who seemed rather conscious of this situation had the following comment:

'Our decision to speak Hungarian at home has had some drawbacks for me. These days I feel less fluent in English than I used to be before the children were born. I wouldn't mind having an au-pair girl, so that I could get out of the house a bit more often, but you can imagine that someone who speaks Hungarian isn't readily available. As the situation stands, there has been little opportunity for me to keep up my English or to improve on it, as was the case when I had my job.'

❝ I must admit that at times I have felt a similar resentment. In my own marriage I am the one who studied English at university and therefore used to have a better command of the language. But since we have moved abroad my husband gets far more practice speaking English in his job than I do, as I am at home for most of the time. Nowadays he regularly receives compliments on his accent and his fluency, even though I have a larger vocabulary and it can still happen that I have to translate a word or expression for him. ❞

But, before I go on, let me make clear that the present discussion of mothers-at-home and working mothers is closely linked with the fact that I am talking about bringing up children to become bilingual rather than about children who grow up bilingually. Mothers who can afford to choose to stay at home when the children are little are in a totally different position to those immigrant mothers who have to take a job in order to survive. The latter group of women will no doubt also experience the influence of the bilingual situation on their own lives and that of their children, but there is hardly much room for choice.

Working mothers

Mothers who stay at home with their children certainly have a choice as to whether or not they want a bilingual upbringing for their children. For mothers who have a full-time job when the children are small, the situation is not quite the same. Geneviève was the first to bring this problem to my notice, as she had this to say about the situation she was in with her daughter:

'My husband used to look after her quite a lot while I was working, and he spoke English to her. The lady who looked after her spoke English to her with an Irish accent and I spoke English with again a different accent. So it was already a bit confusing and I didn't think it was a very good idea to start speaking French to her when I arrived home at six o'clock. The main thing was to communicate with her and the language was secondary.'

As I mentioned before, I didn't meet too many foreign mothers who had a job when the children were young and very few of them worked full-time. But there were others who worked part-time or took a course at a university. Those mothers were rather more in a position to consider the possibility of teaching their children their own language.

❢ I am one of those part-time mothers myself. A dilemma I have had to face is to find a suitable help for the children, such as an au-pair girl or a local childminder. For again the problem of language arises, as a local help will speak the local language and an au-pair is supposed to learn it. Fortunately, until the children started to go to school full-time, I always succeeded in finding Dutch girls who came to live with us and who helped looking after the children. And because of them the children got enough practice speaking Dutch, even though I was not around myself all the time. ❢

As a matter of fact, quite a few of the families I visited had an au-pair or had had one in the past. But only one or two families had opted for a girl who communicated with the children in the same foreign language as the mother or both parents.

As the children get older, the number of mothers in bilingual families who have a job, whether part-time or full-time, increases considerably. Not surprisingly, many of them have jobs in which the use of their original language plays a role. English women especially always stand a fair chance of ending up teaching English as a foreign language. And many women with such jobs told me that it has actually helped them to keep up or to brush up their command of their own mother tongue.

Giving credit

Living with children means living with conflict situations. One can safely say that mothers who stay at home with the children experience a great deal more of that than fathers. Some mothers, however, happily take things in their stride. Madelon seemed to be one of them, for she said:

'As far as having two languages around, it means that I am constantly correcting their use of one or the other. But anyway, that is the kind of stuff that bringing up children is about. And as long as I can see they benefit from it, I don't really mind at all.'

But not only do many mothers feel more responsible, I think that society expects them to feel more responsible. Therefore they are also bound to be the ones who are criticized if problems arise.

❛As my own husband often works at home, his role in keeping up our mother tongue with the children would appear to be the same as mine, for we just all speak Dutch all of the time. The main difference between myself and my husband with respect to our roles in the bilingual upbringing is not so much that I think more about the subject – for in our case that isn't too surprising – but that I used to get far more comments from playleaders and neighbours on the children's slow progress in English. So, while it was our joint decision to keep up the Dutch language, I have been the person who is made to feel more responsible for the children's development in English.

I must add that since the children have become more fluent in English, I am also the one who is more often receiving the compliments on their progress.❜

So, while I believe that mothers bear the brunt of a bilingual upbringing, I also think that – if mothers are successful in bringing up the children bilingually – they deserve to be complimented on it.

10
The role of fathers

After a chapter on the role of mothers in the bilingual upbringing of children, the obvious sequel is a chapter on the role of fathers. But it took me longer to come to grips with this particular aspect. One reason for this was probably that I didn't get a chance to speak to many fathers on their own. The fact that a father volunteered to be interviewed already seemed to indicate that he was interested in the subject. In most cases, however, this meant that I interviewed the parents as a couple. Similarly, of the questionnaires that were returned to me, only a few had been filled in by a father.

One consequence of the fact that relatively few fathers volunteered to be interviewed is that part of my information on the role of fathers comes from mothers. But the picture that seems to emerge is that because fathers spend less time with their children this has a considerable impact on their role in the bilingual upbringing. And, in those cases where they do take an active part in the whole matter, fathers seem to be involved in a different way. Last but not least, an important point with regard to the role of the father – whether he is away from home a lot or takes a more active part in bringing up his children – is that he is someone with whom his children will want to identify at different stages in their bilingual development.

Lack of interest

One explanation for the lack of response from fathers could be that they are not terribly interested in the bilingual development of their offspring, and in some cases this seemed indeed to be the case. The following remark was made by an English mother who lives in Holland and is married to a Dutchman. She wrote:

'I, as mother, attach more importance to teaching the children English and make more effort to do so. Joost thinks little about it and does little, although in theory he is in favour of them learning English to a high level.'

In the case of a mixed-language marriage where the wife comes from abroad, it is not very surprising that she is the person most interested and involved in the problem. But if both partners come from the same foreign country, one might expect that the problems of a bilingual upbringing are at least equally relevant to the father, but again this need not always be the case.

In the next instance husband and wife both come from Cyprus, but they have lived in England all their married life. Actually, the husband had come to England long before they met in order to go to university and start a new career. I spoke to the wife and she told me:

'He speaks both English and Greek better than I do. Yet he seems far less interested than I am in teaching the children both languages. It is my wish that the children should learn Greek and I regularly have to remind my husband to keep it up as the language of the house.'

Lack of time

In another case where the parents also have a single-language marriage the mother had the following observation:

'Because he is away from home an awful lot these days, he says he wants to be good friends with his children when he is there. It means that he doesn't want to watch out for their or his own language use, for he says that his main objective is to communicate with his children.'

In order to communicate with one's children in whatever language, one has to be around. The fact is that many fathers spend long hours away from home and see rather little of their children, especially when the children are small. So for a lot of fathers it is lack of time rather than lack of interest which makes them unable to take part in the bilingual upbringing of their children.

The time when the children are young is often the time when a father is busy establishing himself in his profession. And living abroad can add to the pressure: a mother may find it especially difficult to find a job when living in a foreign country, but a father who lives abroad often does so in pursuit of his career. However, in mixed-language marriages where the father is the only parent who speaks the foreign language his involvement in the bilingual upbringing is essential. Let us now look at how a number of fathers approached this situation.

This father comes from Greece, while his wife has English as her mother tongue. They have three young children and the family live in London. He commented:

'I wish I had been more consistent, but I wouldn't have done it differently though. I have always been too busy with work and, except for weekends, I don't see my children during the day. It doesn't come naturally "time-wise", although recently I have started to make a conscious effort to teach them some Greek.'

Bruno was born and raised in Switzerland and German is his mother tongue, while his wife is French. They live in France and they have two children of seven and five years old. I have talked about them before, in the chapter on children of primary school age. He wrote:

'Theoretically, we did have the choice to teach them either French or German. But since they were born in France, and since the mother tongue of their own mother is French, we could not imagine teaching them German as the first language.'

And as an answer to the question whether he had a different role to his wife, he wrote:

'I think so. Since I am less with our children than my wife, I can spend only little time with them. So I mainly communicate in French with them. When I am more available, i.e. during weekends, we teach German to them.'

Language lessons

A mother who wants her children to know her own language usually speaks this language to them as part of daily life. But if a father decides that his children should learn his original mother tongue, it more often becomes a matter of teaching them the language, which then seems to take place in a different kind of setting. A father may be putting time aside for this purpose, especially during the weekend, thus making the 'language lessons' into special occasions. A walk in the park, taking the children for an outing, reading a story, listening to a record, all these are ways and means that can be used by a father to teach his language to his children.

Even so, a bilingual upbringing is not easy for a father who is the only parent from abroad. Moreover, he might not particularly like the idea of 'language lessons'. Alain is French and he is married to an English wife. They have lived in London for a long time now and their little son is three years old. Both Alain and his wife were present when I arrived to do my interview. Alain told me:

'I know it is up to me to speak French with him and I would feel more close in the long run if he mastered the language. The time to do this would be when I am on my own with him. But often I simply forget, even when I take him to the park on my own at the weekend!

'Right now it feels more important that he gets an idea of "Frenchness" through me. Learning the language should never become a chore, and I would rather he ate some French food and got to know some French songs.'

As a matter of fact, I got the impression that his wife was more anxious about the bilingual upbringing than Alain himself, and this was confirmed when she said:

'I think that I am more worried actually, and sometimes I remind Alain that he should speak French. I have thought about mixing the two languages more myself, but I am afraid that the French he would learn from me would not be very good.'

Identification

If the father is the only parent who comes from abroad, how important is it that the children should learn to speak his language? Will he feel cut off if they don't? It is probably more difficult for a father to make his children speak his own language but, if he doesn't even begin to try, one result might be some unexpected gaps in the way he can relate to his children or they to him.

This father is Dutch and he is married to an English wife. They have lived in England ever since they got married and their sons are eleven and eight years old. He said:

'Although I don't regret my original decision not to teach my sons my own language, I have been finding out recently that my own two boys have no picture of me as a young boy: they don't know the school, or even the sort of school I went to, they don't know the games I used to play, they just know very little of my background. In fact, I feel I myself am forgetting a lot of childhood memories, simply because there is no one I can share them with or who can remind me of them.'

Language is for communication and it helps build relationships. Knowing someone's language means knowing that person better and without such knowledge the relationship may somehow be less complete. These boys don't know their father's native tongue but neither have they been to his country of origin very often. So, in order to develop some understanding of their father's background plus a basic knowledge of his language, plans were being made for the boys to visit their father's country of origin more regularly.

So far, we have seen that some fathers decided not to teach their children their own language, while others reserved a special time to do so. There are also fathers who make an attempt to speak the language as much as possible and who have adopted the one-person-one-language method, as discussed in Chapter 5. I think this method is less common in marriages where the father is the partner from abroad, but it can be done, as is shown by these parents. He is German and his wife's mother tongue is English. They have lived in

England for fourteen years and their children were born in this country. He told me:

'Before the children were born, our language of communication was very much a mixture of German and English. Then, when our first son was born, we made a conscious decision that I would speak German with him, and my wife English. But, in our personal set-up, the fact that each of us speaks a different language with the children has certainly had one major drawback. At a time when our marriage was pretty rotten, it was a way of digging our heels in. It also has meant that, by using one language or the other, the boys were forced to take sides.'

Somewhat to my surprise, it was a father who was the first and also the only one who touched upon this possible consequence of the one-person-one-language strategy, but I think it is quite a significant observation. It shows that language is not an isolated phenomenon and that it influences relationships in all sorts of ways. I think it also shows once again that flexibility and common sense are more important in a bilingual upbringing than the strict application of rules or strategies.

In any mixed-language marriage where each parent speaks his or her own language with the children, there comes a time when a child begins to realize the difference between the two languages spoken by the parents. In the next case it was the mother who spoke the foreign language, and the child's wish to identify with the language of the father, and of the world outside the house, became quite strong at an early age.

Anke is a Dutch friend who lives in Greece with her Greek husband. Her children are now thirteen and twelve years old. She filled in the questionnaire and sent it back to me together with a long letter. She wrote:

'When the children were born, I used to speak Dutch to them, while Kostas spoke Greek to me and the children. Their first words were Dutch, and I remember that the first bedtime stories were also in Dutch, because they understood it better than Greek. As soon as our son, who is the oldest, began to understand that I was the only person who spoke this particular language and that I couldn't use it with anybody else, he rejected it. From then onwards he preferred to wait and learn the Greek word rather than use the Dutch word he already knew. Maybe being a boy had something to do with it? Maybe he was trying to imitate his father, who only spoke Greek?'

Practising at home

Generally speaking, the partner who comes from abroad will learn to speak the language of his or her spouse and for most couples with a mixed-language marriage the local language is the language of communication between the partners. When children begin to arrive and the parents decide on a bilingual upbringing, it is the 'foreign' parent who then starts to use his or her own language again, while the 'local' parent continues to speak the local language, often because that is the only language he or she masters.

But there are also 'local' parents who do speak the foreign language and the couple may then decide to use one language at home, while the other one is mostly reserved for communication with the world outside. A typical example would be a woman marrying someone who is a teacher of the language she was brought up with: a French wife and an English husband who is a teacher of French, while the couple live in England. We have actually come across such a couple in Chapter 3, where we talked about parents who chose a bilingual upbringing as 'a matter of taste'.

The following example, however, shows that a father who is not a professional language teacher may still like to practise the foreign language at home and participate in this way in the bilingual upbringing of his children. Christina comes from England, lives in Spain, and has a Spanish husband. Their two sons are five and two-and-a-half years old. She wrote:

'When we first met we spoke a mixture of Spanish and English with perhaps English dominating slightly, but this very quickly changed to all Spanish and has continued, although when we are speaking to the children we generally both speak English. Still, his English is much weaker than his Spanish and he never uses it in his professional life.

'I felt at the beginning that my husband should speak Spanish to the children as it was his mother tongue, plus because I didn't want them to pick up his faulty pronunciation/grammar. However, he wanted to practise and improve his English by talking to them – I felt this was a bit selfish – but as a matter of fact his English has improved. The children, while making some grammar mistakes from time to time, don't seem to make the ones their father makes, but more from the interference of Spanish – so I have accepted the situation.'

These two children are still fairly young and it is not yet possible to predict their bilingual development in the long run. But it seems that up till now the parents are fairly satisfied with the results and that the children's difficulties in adapting to their all-Spanish environment have not been too big, in spite of the fact that when the older one started nursery school at age two-and-a-half he spoke no Spanish at all and understood only a little.

Still, it is clear that the mother's responsibility in this whole process is considerably larger than the father's. Christina noted this about the difference in roles between herself and her husband:

'I spend more actual hours with the children than my husband does. Also English is my mother tongue, whereas my husband's English is not bad but not wonderful either. I read a lot to them, and talk to them a lot! I think the reading is very important. His relationship with the children is more of the "physical/boisterous game" type than the very articulate.'

Sharing

Although a number of parents acknowledged a difference in roles, some parents, mothers as well as fathers, were obviously both very involved and were sharing the responsibility for the bilingual upbringing. One mother wrote that she and her husband had more or less the same role 'even if the children spend more time with me (till school age and after) than with their father'. A rather typical answer was given by another mother who responded to my question on the difference in roles like this:

'Yes, I have a different role, but not as a mother. Being French and of a French culture, I am more qualified to pass on to my children my French culture and my language.'

And her husband added:

'The same would be true of my role as an English speaker.'

Interestingly, one mother noted a shift in her feelings with respect to sharing the responsibility. She is English, her husband is French, and they live in France. She said:

'When the children were young, I thought it was entirely up to me to teach them English, as I am the one who comes from England. Lately I have come to realize that, if he finds it important for them to become bilingual, he should take his share. His English isn't bad at all and we could make an effort to speak English during mealtimes for instance. Now, if we don't succeed in doing so, I no longer feel I am the only one who is, or should be held, responsible for it.'

I think that her remark illustrates a number of points that have been raised in this and the previous chapter. And I also think that – however one sees the different roles of fathers and mothers in a bilingual upbringing – eventually parents can and should share the load.

11
Reactions of other people

'At the time when I was trying to bring up my children with two languages, I usually met with resistance from the people around me and their advice would be to stop confusing my children. In due course I did give up talking Dutch to them and consequently my children can only speak Greek. Nowadays people again offer their opinion, but this time they will say, "Why on earth didn't you teach your children your own language?"'

This is the experience of Anke, the Dutch friend who wrote to me from Greece. It demonstrates that, whatever decision parents have made with respect to the bilingual upbringing of their children, it never seems right in the eyes of the outside world. A few parents told me that in their view there is a general lack of interest in this subject. Others were convinced that people don't care what language you speak at home, providing you keep it private. But my main impression is that Anke's experience is fairly typical. For most parents agree that there is an almost constant stream of comments, advice, criticism, and warnings, which are bound to affect them in some way or other.

Who are they?

What do other people know about bilingual children? It appears that this is one of those subjects about which a lot of people think they know something. Moreover, they are always volunteering this knowledge. One of the mothers I talked to complained:

'There are many self-appointed experts around, but the advice people give you is never very helpful, even if it is only meant to reassure you that there needn't be any problems.'

Let us have a closer look at who those people are and at the things they are telling parents. First of all, the category of 'other people' is too wide and therefore it makes sense to distinguish between neighbours, acquaintances, friends, relatives, and schoolteachers. They all play a part in parents' lives and they all have their different reasons for commenting on a particular course of action in the bilingual situation.

Neighbours and acquaintances usually do not have a personal interest in the bilingual development of one's children, while relatives and schoolteachers have. I will talk about the last two groups later, but first we will have a look at the comments parents regularly get from local people. And at the end of this chapter I will discuss the reactions of friends.

It's never right

When someone overhears you talking a foreign language to your child, he or she often gets curious and asks you what language you are speaking and whether the child is bilingual. Especially when children are small, it is often thought to be rather endearing that they speak a foreign language. And it isn't threatening yet, for a conversation with small children is more or less the same in any language and people can often guess what you are saying to your child. Even so, reactions aren't favourable all of the time.

David is English and his wife comes from the French-speaking part of Belgium. They live in Holland and they have two small girls. We read about the successful start of their bilingual upbringing in Chapter 6. David also wrote:

'Most people think it's rather good that we have a child who seems to have little problem with two languages. One person was against it for ideological/social reasons (didn't think it would work in terms of the child being socially accepted), but has since changed her opinion when these problems don't seem to have arisen.'

But he also stated:

'Some people, chance acquaintances usually, have attitudes bordering on the aggressive about how these kids of ours will have trouble fitting in later – at school etc.'

Things tend to get more serious when the children are no longer toddlers and are approaching school age. All of a sudden, people around you can start making comments with far-reaching implications, although they themselves might not quite realize this. Jonneke and her husband are both Dutch and they live near London. She recalled:

'People who live locally have been telling me that I should be speaking English to my children instead of Dutch. But if I ask them whether they would speak French to their children if they moved to France, they react with an indignant "no, of course not".'

If one keeps a record of all the questions and comments, one soon discovers a curious dichotomy. The opinion held in general seems to be that it is very easy for young children to learn a second language. At the same time, people are very ready to point out that children get confused very quickly and that bilingual children don't learn either language very well.

All parents who live with the bilingual experience have come across these varying opinions. But some parents come in for more criticism than others. Take for instance those parents who try to keep up a language with their children that is not regarded as being very 'useful', such as Norwegian or Dutch. They are regarded with far more suspicion than parents who have created a bilingual French–English situation. So, if parents insist on a bilingual upbringing for their children, the languages involved had better be useful ones, for otherwise the parents are not infrequently considered to be selfish.

A distinction is also made between parents in mixed-language marriages and couples who have migrated together. In the latter case people are more willing to accept that parents want to keep up their own language, even if they will regularly remind those parents that the children should have sufficient chance to assimilate the local language. Parents in a mixed-language marriage, where one or both parents speak a foreign language with their children, are more often looked upon as striving after peculiar ideals. Why would they want to make their children different from the others? What's good enough for the rest – to know only one language – should be good enough for them.

But, in whatever situation one lives, or whatever choice one has made with regard to the bilingual upbringing of one's children, people love to comment. Ulla comes from Germany, but both her children were born and raised in England and have an English father. She had this to say about it:

'Whenever people ask me whether I have taught my children to speak German, and I say "No!", they will say "What a shame!" or "My god, you missed a chance!" With time I have learned to reply with "I think that's debatable", and then leave the matter at that.'

There is one group of parents who may expect more reassuring comments from the people around them than any other group, at least for a while. Those are the parents who have recently migrated to a new country with their children, a position we used to be in ourselves.

❛ When we came to England, Hedda and Gideon were eighteen months and almost three years old. After a few months, when the hustle of moving house and settling in a new country had died down a bit, people began to enquire how the children were learning to speak English. And invariably we were assured by everyone around us that from now on their English would develop quickly and naturally.

But, as a matter of fact, it didn't, and when it still didn't after more than a year, those remarks that were meant to be kind and reassuring – such as "All young children learn a new language quickly and easily." – began to have the opposite effect. 〟

No doubt, parents learn to live with the comments and criticisms of the people around them. But I'm sure they all agree with Judy, who said:

'The only people who know what it takes to bring up your children with two languages are the ones who have actually gone through the process themselves. All the others just haven't got a clue.'

Schools and schoolteachers

Although unsolicited advice from neighbours and other local people isn't always welcome or helpful, it doesn't need to bother or influence parents too much in what they do. It starts to matter, though, when parents receive comments from the schools to which they are sending their children.

〟 One month after we had arrived in London, I dutifully went around the corner with three-year-old Gideon to put his name on the waiting-list of the local school. "You'd better make sure he is speaking English by the time he starts here", was the remark I was to bring home with me. "Yes, of course", I answered, but I immediately wondered what they would do if he didn't. 〟

The point about schools is that parents are so dependent on them as to how they treat their bilingual children. Nowadays there are many schools and schoolteachers with some experience of children who speak a different language at home. It often seems that the actual experience of having had to teach children who either did well or did not do well as a result of their bilingualism determines the schoolteacher's attitude towards new pupils. This is in itself not too surprising, but it shows that there is no general rule or consensus on how to deal with bilingual children. And another result of this is that as a parent one never knows what to expect.

Many parents actually report that their children have absolutely no difficulties at school. In some cases they tell me that teachers had even encouraged them to practise reading and writing in the other language at home, as it was thought that it would enhance the children's language awareness. If, on the other hand, the child shows even one sign of being slightly behind, the blame is all too easily put on the bilingual situation. Marie-Luce remembered the following example:

'Maxime appeared to have problems with reading at school and just before the Christmas holidays the teacher told us to stop speaking French to him at home. Of course we didn't, but we did sit down with him to read in English. When he went back after the holidays, it soon became clear that he had caught up with the rest of his class. The teacher triumphantly told us that apparently her remedy had worked.'

Schoolteachers can't always be blamed for not knowing how to cope with bilingual children, for it seems to me that they suffer from the same lack of information as everybody else. Lack of information needn't be an excuse for a lack of common sense though. Judy said she became rather angry at what she thought was bad conduct on behalf of the teacher. She told me:

'At home we speak English and it has taken Sarah a long time to learn Dutch. She is a bit shy and doesn't always communicate easily with other people. One day I fetched her from nursery school and overheard the teacher say to her "You won't get this back unless you ask for it in Dutch." That same teacher had spoken both English and Dutch to her ever since Sarah started there. I thought it was in rather bad taste and even cruel that all of a sudden a rule was set for a small child that didn't seem to apply to the teacher herself.'

Grandparents and other relatives

When we think about relatives and their reactions to the bilingual situation in which we live, the grandparents come first to mind. To them, of course, it is of great importance to be able to communicate with their grandchildren. Not that all grandparents can be or want to be around all that often. It depends on age, health, travelling distance, money, the overall number of grandchildren, and what have you. But provided there is regular contact with the grandparents, language will undoubtedly play a role.

In the case of mixed-language marriages, the grandparents on either side will anxiously watch which language or languages will be spoken by the grandchildren. And in the case of couples who have migrated together, the issue at stake for the grandparents is how long will the original mother tongue be preserved.

Grandparents, like any other people, have their information on the subject, or lack of it, and this will influence their reactions. They may be afraid that the children will become confused, or they think it all ought to be a matter of course, or they are disappointed in the results.

In all those cases where the parents have come from a bilingual background, the grandparents obviously have some personal experience in the matter. This fact may make the grandparents more understanding or more demanding, but either way they are relying on memories which may have become unreliable with time. Being in the middle of a situation is always different from looking back on it, and circumstances are never the same anyhow.

There are also grandparents who will try to find out more about the subject of bilingual children, for their own sake or at their children's request, as was pointed out to me by my own mother. She used to work in a large public library in Amsterdam and she told me that on several occasions she had had the following request for information: 'My daughter lives abroad and now that she has a baby she wonders what language she should speak with the child. She wrote me a letter asking me to buy a book about this subject, but as they couldn't help me in the bookshop, I decided to come to the library.' And, at the time, my mother always had to tell these people that there was no such book available for parents – or for grandparents – who have to cope with a bilingual situation.

As I mentioned before in Chapter 8, I found that many of the parents I talked to had brothers and sisters who had also got married to someone from abroad or who had moved abroad themselves. One would suppose that it would be nice to share one's experiences with such close relatives, but the respective situations often differ a lot, and so do the opinions.

Theresa is English, while she lives in France and has a French husband. She wrote:

'My brother is married to an Italian and their children were brought up in Italy and learnt English only at school. He invariably pleads that fathers don't spend enough time with their children, so it's not worthwhile bringing them up to be bilingual – unless they hope to return to their homeland with their family. Nevertheless, he finds it quite normal to be able to communicate with my children in English.'

Old and new friends

And now we come to the reactions of friends. Unlike relatives or schoolteachers, they do not have a personal stake in the bilingual development of one's children. But they are certainly more inclined to be genuinely interested in the matter than mere acquaintances.

Friends come in all sorts. If you live in a foreign country, you could make a distinction between old friends 'back home' and new local friends. The latter category can then be divided into people who are born and raised in the country where you are living now and people who are foreigners themselves. These three groups of friends tend to react differently to the way parents choose to bring up their children as far as language is concerned.

Life-long friends back home are usually most supportive. If your children are bilingual, they think it is great. If you give up or haven't even tried, they will also understand. One reason for their tolerance might be that if they are capable of understanding and speaking one or two foreign languages themselves, they may quite like practising these languages in conversations with their friends' children!

Also, having friends who live in a foreign country may supply a nice excuse for going there on a holiday or for sending one's children to learn the other language. In the latter case, a successful bilingual upbringing may even spoil some of the fun. The following observation came from Françoise:

'Now that the children are getting somewhat older, we have exchanges with the children of my friends in France. But the French children who come to stay with us in London don't practise their English enough really, for my own children will just as easily converse with them in French.'

New friends whom one meets among local people are often not more than superficially interested in one's struggle with languages. The subject is always good for some small talk, and in the best of cases one is admired for the effort, but soon the conversation will continue along more interesting lines. In general, the way to bring up children is an inexhaustible topic for parents, but, as far as children's language development is concerned, families who live in a monolingual situation have little in common with those who live in a bilingual setting.

A common interest

The third category of friends are those who are foreigners themselves. Bilingual families are bound to meet other bilingual families who happen to live nearby. Whether or not parents are actively looking for other parents who come from abroad, sooner or later their paths will cross. Some of the other expatriates will become friends, and a common interest will be the bilingual upbringing of the children. However, a common interest needn't imply a common policy, as Tjitske told me. She and her husband came from Holland to live near London some five years ago. According to her:

'It all depends on who is considered to be the "expert". Parents with younger children will sometimes ask me how I cope. Other mothers regard themselves as more successful in keeping up both languages and tell me I'm not strict enough. We all draw our lines differently and we all have very much our own way of dealing with the bilingual situation.'

Still, I believe that parents living with children in a bilingual situation should share their experiences. This is easier for those who live in a large metropolitan area, where there are bound to be more expatriates, than for those who live in smaller, more secluded communities. Yet, a sense of isolation – the feeling that one is the only person with this particular problem – may at times be experienced by any parent or child, wherever the family live.

I hope that this book will help parents and children feel less isolated, and that it will make them realize that to be or to become bilingual is in fact a common interest to many millions of people all over the world.

Postscript

It is now six-and-a-half years since we left Holland and almost four-and-a-half years since we settled in London. In the process of learning to live with two languages, I myself have greatly benefited from the conversations I had with other parents. I asked many people many questions and I learned a lot from their answers.

When I first started writing this book, I had many doubts and worries about the bilingual development of Gideon and Hedda. Also, at the time, my own bilingual experience was still quite brief and so was my experience as a parent. These two circumstances added to my feelings of uncertainty, and all this is no doubt reflected in the book.

But by sharing my feelings and experiences with other parents in similar circumstances, my sense of isolation and frustration has all but disappeared. Moreover, as my children's confidence to express themselves in English has increased considerably over the past year – while they still speak Dutch quite well – my own confidence has grown that it is in fact possible to bring up one's children with two languages, with everybody gaining from the experience.

London, December 1985

The photograph on the back cover shows the author and her husband with Gideon and Hedda, then aged four and a half and three.

Questionnaire for parents

1 a In which language(s) did you and your partner communicate when you first got to know each other, and has this changed over the years?

  b Which language(s) do you speak at your job and in your social life?
    Has this changed over the years?

  c Which language(s) does your partner speak at his/her job and in his/her social life? Has this changed over the years?

2 a Would you describe yourself as being 'bilingual'?
    If yes, why? If not, why not?

  b Has your fluency in your mother tongue changed over the years?

  c Would you describe your partner as being 'bilingual'?
    If yes, why? If not, why not?

  d Has his/her fluency in his/her mother tongue changed over the years?
    Please distinguish between understanding/speaking/reading/writing.

3 a Do you feel you had a choice when the children were born (or when you migrated) as to which language(s) you wanted to teach them?

  b If yes, what were your reasons for making a particular choice?

  c If not, why not?

4   Which language(s) have you and your partner been speaking to the children:

  a before they started going to school?

  b since they started going to school?

  c Has the situation been the same for different children?
    Please give particulars.

5 a Do you have special rules for dealing with two languages in your home?

  b Have you come across any particular problems concerning the bilingual situation in your home?

6 a Would you describe your children as being, or in the process of becoming, 'bilingual'?

96

If yes, why? If not, why not?
Please distinguish between understanding/speaking/reading/
writing.

b   In your opinion, what are the advantages of being brought up
    bilingually?

c   In your opinion, what are the disadvantages of being brought
    up bilingually?

7   a   In the case of young children (or when the children were
        young), do/did they ever make comments on the fact that they
        can/could speak or have/had to speak two different languages?

    b   Do you think they have ever felt different from other children
        for that reason?

    c   Have they ever experienced particular problems in their contact
        with other children?

8   a   How often have you visited your or your partner's country of
        origin?

    b   How often have you had visitors from your or your partner's
        country of origin?

9   a   Do you as a mother/father have a different role in the bilingual
        upbringing of your children than your partner in his/her role
        as a father/mother?
        Please give particulars.

10 a   Have you ever talked with other people about your experiences
        or problems concerning a bilingual upbringing?
        If yes, what have been the reactions of:

    b   other parents who live abroad and whose children are
        bilingual?

    c   other parents who live abroad and whose children are not
        bilingual?

    d   relatives?

    e   schools?

    f   other people, such as friends and neighbours?

11 a   Apart from talking to other people, what sources of
        information on bilingualism have been available to you, for
        instance, books, magazines, television?

    b   Would you agree that the opinion held by the 'general public'
        is that learning a second language comes quickly and easily for
        young children?

    c   Do you agree with that opinion yourself?

Notes:
General remarks:
Other subjects:

Questionnaire for teenagers

1   a   Would you describe yourself as being 'bilingual'?
If yes, why? If not, why not?
Please distinguish between understanding/speaking/reading/writing.

     b   If you don't consider yourself to be bilingual, do you think you would have liked to be so?
If yes, why? If not, why not?

2   a   How did you learn to speak two different languages?

     b   How much of the two languages is still spoken at home?

     c   Do you remember whether there have been any 'house rules' for keeping the two languages apart?

3   a   In your opinion, what are the advantages of being brought up bilingually?

     b   In your opinion, what are the disadvantages of being brought up bilingually?

     c   Do you think that once you have learned two languages, it is easier to learn a third or fourth language?

4   a   Do you think that learning a different language is just a matter of learning new words, or do you think that you also learn something about a different culture? Can you give me an example?

     b   Do you think you can learn something about another culture without learning the other language? Can you give me an example?

5   a   Do you like travelling?

     b   If you had a choice, in which country would you prefer to live, now and in the future?

6   a   Being bilingual or having bilingual parents, has it made you feel different from other children?
If yes, why?

     b   Do you know any other bilingual children?

     c   Have you ever talked to them about how it feels to be bilingual?

     d   Can you remember other people's reactions to your being bilingual (or not bilingual)?

7   a   Finally, if you had children of your own, would you like them to become bilingual?
If yes, why? If not, why not?

Further reading

Many academic articles and books have been published on the subject of bilingual children and bilingualism in general. The following list is a personal selection of fairly recent publications (with one exception). Interested readers should be able to make themselves familiar with the study of bilingualism through these books, most of which contain extensive bibliographies.

Baetens Beardsmore, Hugo. *Bilingualism: Basic Principles*. Multilingual Matters, 1982
An introduction to bilingualism that was first conceived and used as a textbook for students. The book claims to be also of interest to parents and educators, but its rather technical approach doesn't make it very accessible to the non-professional reader.
Grosjean, François. *Life with Two Languages. An Introduction to Bilingualism*. Harvard University Press, 1982
A comprehensive treatment of the study of bilingualism presented in an attractive format with many first-hand reports of bilingual persons. This book is basically a textbook and is written for professionals and students in linguistics, education, sociology, and psychology, but it may appeal to anyone seriously interested in bilingualism.
Leopold, W. F. *Speech Development of a Bilingual Child: A Linguist's Record*, 4 vols. Northwestern University Press, 1939–49
The classic example of a meticulously recorded case study of bilingual development concerning the author's daughter Hildegard. Often quoted in writings on bilingual children.
McLaughlin, Barry. *Second-Language Acquisition in Childhood*. Lawrence Erlbaum Associates, 1978
This book gives a very useful and interesting overview of the academic literature on how children acquire a second language. It not only describes research that has been carried out so far, but also indicates where research still needs to be done and exposes some common misconceptions about bilingual development in children.
Miller, Jane, *Many Voices. Bilingualism, Culture and Education*. Routledge & Kegan Paul, 1983
The prime focus of this book is education, as the author puts forward linguistic, pedagogic, and political arguments towards the development of a multicultural curriculum. It concludes a couple of interviews with bilingual speakers and a final chapter on writing in a second language by world-famous novelists.

Further reading

Rosen, Harold, and Burgess, Tony. *Languages and Dialects of London Schoolchildren. An Investigation.* Ward Lock, 1980
Account of a research project carried out in twenty-eight inner-London secondary schools. This book makes fairly technical reading, but it does give an interesting picture of all the changes that have taken place as a traditionally monolinguistic society is being transformed into a multilinguistic society.

Rabel-Heymann, Lili. 'But How Does a Bilingual Feel? Reflections on Linguistic Attitudes of Immigrant Academics.' In: Paradis, M. (ed.). *Aspects of Bilingualism.* Hornbaum Press, 1978, pp. 220–8
The only article I came across that deals with the emotions of bilingual speakers rather than with linguistic phenomena. The paper describes a limited research project (21 respondents answered 25 yes/no questions), but offers plenty material for identification.

Saville-Troike, Muriel. *The Ethnography of Communication. An Introduction.* Basil Blackwell, 1982
This book does not strictly deal with the study of bilingualism, but makes worthwhile reading for anyone interested in how and why language is used and how its use varies in different cultures. With many references to linguistic research and lots of fascinating examples concerning linguistic diversity.

Saunders, George. *Bilingual Children: Guidance for the Family.* Multilingual Matters, 1982
An Australian father describes the bilingual development of his two sons and the positive results are meant to encourage other parents who are contemplating raising their children bilingually. In spite of references to other research on bilingual children, the scope of this book remains rather limited and the endless accounts of the two children's linguistic performances become a bit boring after a while.

Wallwark, J. F. *Language and People.* Heinemann Educational Books, 1978
A very readable introduction to the complex relationship between language and people, including a chapter on bilingual and multilingual communities. The book avoids technical terminology, while still explaining many of the relevant notions in the study of sociolinguistics.